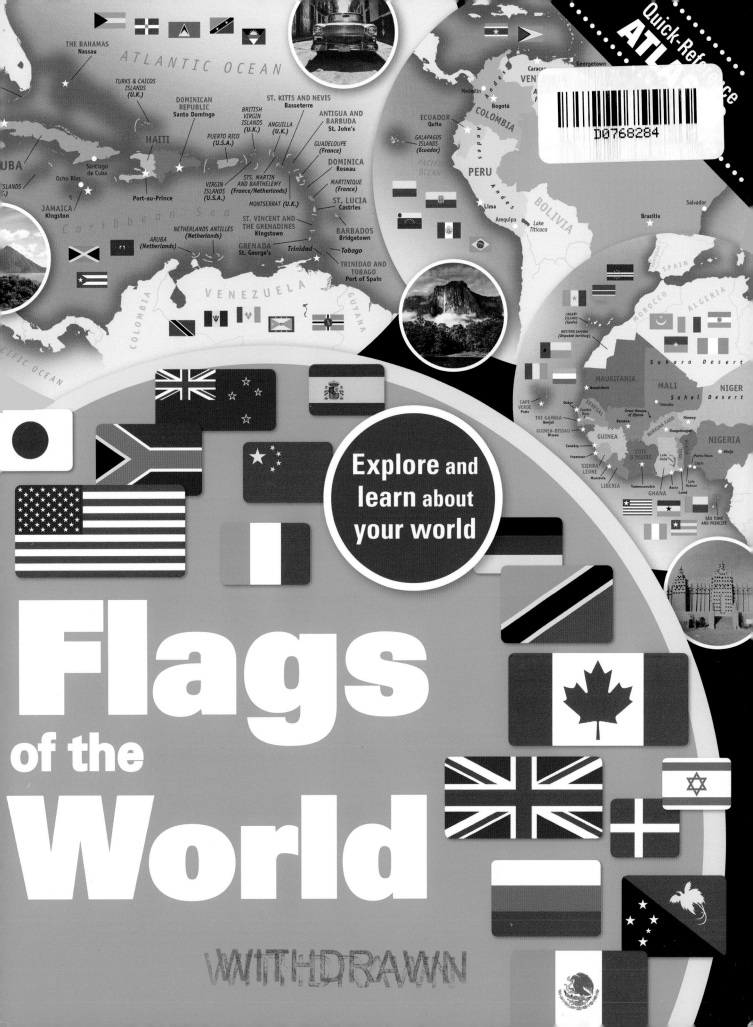

Flags
of the
World

Explore and learn about your world

D0768284

Author:
Lyn Coutts

Editorial director:
Kathy Middleton

Editor:
Wendy Scavuzzo

Proofreader:
Rodelinde Albrecht

Cover and interior design:
Green Android Ltd

Print and production coordinator:
Katherine Berti

Sources:
World Factbook
CIA; World Bank;
and Department
of Economic and
Social Affairs,
United Nations

Images © shutterstock.com: Abu Dhabi © JoemanjiArts, Alexandria Library © Baloncici, American flag © Rudy Balasko, Ancient theatre, Bulgaria © Bildagentur Zoonar GmbH, Angel Falls © Alice Nerr, Coffee berries © bonga1965, Auschwitz © Caminoel, Australian flag © Jim Barber, Avenida 9 de Julio © meunierd, Bauxite mine © Roberto Lucci, Bibi-Khanym Mosque © eFesenko, Brunei's water village © Sophie James, Cameroon children © Michal Szymanski, Caribbean beach © Ramona Heim, Car in Havana © Kamira, Chinese flag © hxdbzxy, Coconut field © napat uthaichai, Colombian flag © Jess Kraft, Crusher © al7, Danish flag © Paul Maguire, "David" sculpture © xamnesiacx, Los Angeles © Sean Pavone, Drilling rig © Richard Goldberg, Netherlands countryside © Sander van der Werf, Japan earthquake house © dailin, Egyptian flag © Jim Barber, Elmina Castle © trevor kittelty, Face mask © debra millet, Fjord © Berzina, Botswanan flag © david n madden, Brazilian flag © Adao, Canadian flag © Muskoka Stock Photos, Irish flag © pasaro, Israeli flag © ULKASTUDIO, Italian flag © Diego Barbieri, Malaysian flag © Adrin Shamsudin, Flags at United Nations HQ © Andrea Izzotti, Smog-bound Beijing © testing, Football match © AGIF, Forbidden City, Beijing © ChameleonsEye, French flag © Mark Herreid, German flag © Johann Helgason, Ghanaian flag © pudiq, Guatemala City shantytown © Charles Harker, Heviz Lake, Hungary © andras_csontos, Hindus in the Ganges © Darko Sikman, Hot air balloon above Melbourne © Nils Versemann, Hillside housing in Port-Au-Prince, Haiti © Glenda, Indian god statue © Anton_Ivanov, Insect © Graham R Prentice, Dead Sea © kavram, Kalgoorlie Super Pit © Glyn Spencer, Lagos Nigeria © Bill Kret, Luxembourg © gevision, Luzzu boat, Malta © Anibal Trejo, Grand Bazaar Istanbul © Alexander Freydin, Maluti Mountains © BarryTuck, Family © Rob Hainer, Moraine Lake, Canada © Zhukova Valentyna, Gorillas © GUDKOV ANDREY, Nelson Mandela © Alessia Pierdomenico, North Korean army © Astrelok, Nutmeg © Arrfoto, Ocho Rios Jamaica © jiawangkun, Old Town Stockholm © Oleksiy Mark, Ortigas and Makati in Manila © donsimon, Pamir Highway, Tajikistan © Jakub Czajkowski, Panama Canal © meunierd, Peanut pickers Senegal © Sviluppo, Petrographs in Azerbaijan © Tonis Valing, Pitons Saint Lucia © PlusONE, Protesters © mavkate, Pyrenees © mbonaparte, Roatan Honduras © Ritu Manoj Jethani, Roman mosaic © ailenn, Vehicle launch © vicspacewalker, Saigon Vietnam © weltreisendertj, San Fermin festival © Migel, Santiago © Pablo Rogat, Shinsegae Department Store South Korea © Keith Homan, Sifaka © Rich Lindie, Singapore dollars © Ashwin, South African flag © Jim Barber, South Korean flag © Rob Wilson, Sri Siva Subramaniya Swami Fiji © Henryk Sadura, Stilt village in Benin © trevor kittelty, Sun temple in the Himalayas © Dariush M, Swedish flag © Andreas Gradin, Somali immigrant tent camp © Sadik Gulec, Thatched houses Swaziland © Gil.K, The BAKER test © Everett Historical, The Big mosque © Michel Piccaya, South African Embassy © Rusty Pelican, Tanah Lot Temple Bali © Aleksandar Todorovic, The White House © David Evison, Mayan ruinsat Tikal © Zai Aragon, Tram in Tallinn © Leonid Andronov, Trans-Siberian Railway © russal, Nuclear cooling towers © prochasson Frederic, Ulaanbaatar © Julia Baturina, Union Jack flag © Diego Barbieri, Volcano in Iceland © Gardar Olafsson, Wind turbine © Johan Swanepoel, Dragonblood trees Socotra Yemen © Ovchinnikova Irina, Zlatni Rat beach Croatia © paul Prescott.

Library and Archives Canada Cataloguing in Publication

Coutts, Lyn, author
    Flags of the world / Lyn Coutts.

(Quick-reference atlases)
Includes index.
Issued in print and electronic formats.
ISBN 978-0-7787-5047-5 (hardcover).--
ISBN 978-0-7787-5050-5 (softcover).--
ISBN 978-1-4271-2149-3 (HTML)

    1. Flags--Juvenile literature. 2. Flags--Miscellanea--Juvenile literature.
I. Title.

CR101.C68 2018   j929.9'2   C2018-902487-9
                                          C2018-902488-7

Library of Congress Cataloging-in-Publication Data

Names: Coutts, Lyn, active 1998, author.
Title: Flags of the world / Lyn Coutts.
Description: New York, New York : Crabtree Publishing Company, [2019] |
    Series: Quick-reference atlases | Includes index.
Identifiers: LCCN 2018021429 (print) | LCCN 2018026372 (ebook) |
    ISBN 9781427121493 (Electronic) |
    ISBN 9780778750475 (hardcover) |
    ISBN 9780778750505 (pbk.)
Subjects: LCSH: Flags--Juvenile literature. | Emblems, National--Juvenile
    literature. | Children's atlases.
Classification: LCC CR101 (ebook) | LCC CR101 .C68 2019 (print) |
    DDC 929.9/2--dc23
LC record available at https://lccn.loc.gov/2018021429

Crabtree Publishing Company

www.crabtreebooks.com   1-800-387-7650

Published in 2019 by Crabtree Publishing Company

Published in Canada
Crabtree Publishing
616 Welland Ave.
St. Catharines, Ontario
L2M 5V6

Published in the United States
Crabtree Publishing
PMB 59051
350 Fifth Avenue, 59th Floor
New York, New York 10118

Created and produced by:
Green Android Ltd
49 Beaumont Court
Upper Clapton Road
London E5 8BG
United Kingdom
www.greenandroid.co.uk

Please note that every effort has been made to check the accuracy of the information contained in this book, and to credit the copyright holders correctly. Green Android Ltd apologise for any unintentional errors or omissions, and would be happy to include revisions to content and/or acknowledgements in subsequent editions of this book.

Printed in the U.S.A./082018/CG20180601

About this atlas

National flags symbolize a country's history, culture, people, and aspirations—its dreams for the future. So, learning about flags is way of gaining greater understanding about countries of the world. This book will help you identify a country's flag, know where the country is located, and be informed about the country. But above all, this book reveals the heroic and tragic stories behind some flag designs.

Key to the maps

Watch for these symbols on the maps. They pinpoint population centers, physical features, and borders.

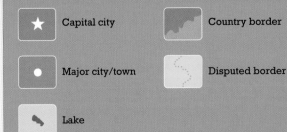

★ Capital city

● Major city/town

◣ Lake

▰ Country border

┅ Disputed border

Contents

4 About flags

6 North and Central America

8 The Caribbean

10 Northern South America

11 Southern South America

12 Northern and Eastern Africa

14 Western Africa

16 Central Africa

17 Southern Africa

18 Northern Europe and Russia

20 Western Europe

21 Eastern Europe

22 Southern Europe

24 Southwest Asia

26 Central Asia

27 South Asia

28 East Asia

30 Southeast Asia

32 Australia, New Zealand, and Pacific Islands

34 Flags at a glance

35 Learning More and Glossary

36 Index

About flags

Flags are flown on official buildings, used to mark special events, and waved to support national teams. They are symbols that represent a people, a nation, or an **ideal**. Ancient peoples did not have flags. Instead, they decorated their shields in a special way to represent their "tribe." Explorers hoist a flag when they claim land for their country, armies march under the flag of their country, and citizens rally around their flag.

Parts of a flag

When designing or hoisting a flag, a strict language is used. Below are some of the words used to describe the parts of a flag.

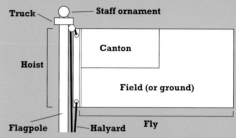

Truck — Staff ornament

Canton

Hoist

Field (or ground)

Flagpole — Halyard — Fly

Flag protocol

There are strict rules governing flags. It is illegal in many countries to burn a national flag in protest and the US flag is never to be used in advertising. Here are some other rules:

- When many national flags are flown together, they must all be hoisted to the same height.
- A host country's flag must be raised and lowered first.
- Flags should always be displayed the right way up.
- Flags should not be flown in bad weather.
- Flags should only be flown sunrise to sunset, unless the flag is brightly lit.
- When a flag is lowered, it can't touch the ground.

Flags outside the United Nations Headquarters in New York

Special rules

- The flag of the Philippines is flown upside down when the country is at war.
- A ship can signal distress by hoisting its flag upside down.
- A flag hung below the top of a flagpole is at half-mast. It means a country is in mourning.

South African flag at half-mast

Flag patterns

The study of flags is called vexillology, from the Latin word for flag, *vexillum*. Flags can change frequently. Sometimes the change is small, but if a country has gained **independence** or changed government, a new flag may be designed. Here are 12 of the most frequently used flag patterns.

Border
This runs around all four edges of the flag and can contain a pattern or images.
Example: Montenegro

Canton
This is the top inner corner of a flag. Stars and Union Jacks are often seen in cantons.
Example: Australia

Quarterly
This is when the flag is divided by two lines to create four rectangles of the same size.
Example: Panama

Greek cross
This cross has four closed arms of equal length. It is a symbol of the Christian church.
Example: Switzerland

Symmetrical cross
The arms meet at the flag's center and extend to the edges of the flag.
Example: Georgia

Scandinavian cross
Also known as the Nordic cross, the arms intersect off-center, toward the hoist.
Example: Norway

Pale
This is a band that runs vertically down the center of a flag. It can vary in width.
Example: Mali

Fess
This is a band that runs horizontally across the center of a flag. It can vary in width.
Example: Armenia

Bicolor
This horizontal, vertical, or diagonal line cuts the flag into two parts, evenly or unevenly.
Example: Bhutan

Chevron
This is a V-shaped pattern. In some forms, it appears as a triangle, in others as a V.
Example: Cuba

Pall
This is a Y-shaped pattern. It can be placed upright, upside down, or on its side.
Example: South Africa

Saltire
This is a diagonal cross, and it is sometimes called the cross of St. Andrew.
Example: Jamaica

Flag sizes

So that a flag looks the same no matter what its size, size is given as a ratio. The most common ratio is 2:3—two units high by three units wide. Most flags are rectangular, but those of Switzerland, Vatican City State, and Nepal are unusual.

2:3 ratio Romanian flag

Qatar's flag is much longer than it is high

The square flags of Switzerland and the Vatican City State

The two triangles of Nepal's flag

State flags

It is not only countries that have flags. States, territories, provinces, and counties also have flags that represent a special or valued aspect of their culture, history, landscape, or industry. Here are some USA and Australian state flags.

United States of America

California
The California grizzly bear represents strength, red stands for courage, white for purity, and the star for sovereignty.

Montana
The landscape speaks of the state's natural beauty and features, while the tools—plow, pickax, and shovel—represent farming and mining.

Washington
Known as the "Evergreen State," it is the only state flag to depict a person. George Washington was the first president of the USA.

Australia

New South Wales
The Union Jack sits in the canton, and in the disk is the St. George Cross. On the cross are a lion (link to the UK), and four eight-pointed stars.

Northern Territory
Black, white, and ocher are the state colors. On them sits the Southern Cross as stars. The petals of Sturt's desert rose are for the territory and six Australian states.

Western Australia
Alongside the Union Jack is a golden disk with a black swan. This **colony** was called Swan River Settlement after the flocks of black swans.

International flags

There are many flags that represent internationally recognized associations. Though these associations may be headquartered in a particular country, their flags symbolize their global mission or ideal.

Secretariat of the Antarctic Treaty

Association of Southeast Asian Nations (ASEAN)

European Union

Paralympic Games

International Red Cross

North Atlantic Treaty Organization (NATO)

Olympic Games

 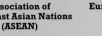

United Nations

United Nations Educational, Scientific and Cultural Organization (UNESCO)

United Nations International Children's Emergency Fund (UNICEF)

Distress flags at sea

When out at sea, people use flags to communicate from their boat or ship. These are some distress flags and their meanings.

S.O.S (Save our souls) and Mayday flag

"You are heading into danger!"

"Man overboard!"

If these two flags are hoisted, it is a distress signal.

Flag records

Oldest design still in use
Dating from 1370, Denmark's flag design is still in use.

Largest flag flown
Mexico's 112.5 ft by 197 ft (34 m by 60 m) flag, hoisted in 2011, broke all records for size.

Most distant flags
There are six US flags planted on the Moon. Five remain standing but the Apollo 11 flag, which cost a mere $5.50 in 1969, was knocked over in 1973 by the force of the exhaust from a departing lunar module.

Tallest flagpole
The world's tallest flagpole is in Jeddah, Saudi Arabia. It is 561 ft (171 m) tall. The flag itself is 108 ft by 162 ft (33 m by 49.5 m).

Highest flags
When Sir Edmund Hillary and Tenzing Norgay reached the summit of Mount Everest in 1953, they planted the flags of the United Kingdom, United Nations, and Nepal. Today, climbers plant national flags or Tibetan prayer flags at Everest Base Camp, which is below the summit.

North and Central America

North America consists of Mexico, the 50 states of the USA, Canada, and the territories of Greenland, St. Pierre and Miquelon, and Bermuda. The seven Central American countries, sitting between the Pacific Ocean and the Caribbean Sea, are subject to hurricanes, floods, and volcanic eruptions. Central America, unlike its wealthier northern neighbors, has much **poverty**. Nicaragua is the second-poorest Western country.

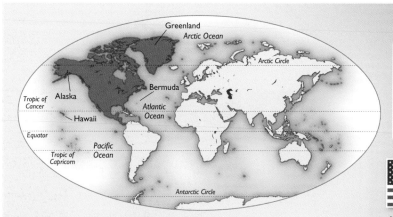

NORTH AMERICA

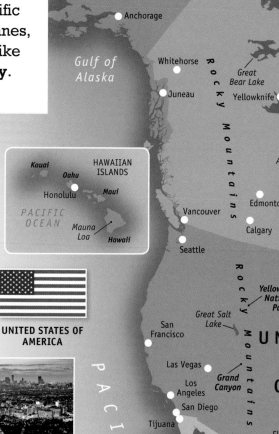

United States of America

Canada
Capital city: Ottawa
Population: 35,623,680
Land area: 3,511,023 mi² (9,093,507 km²)
Population density: 10 per mi² (4 per km²)

Mexico
Capital city: Mexico City
Population: 124,574,795
Land area: 750,561 mi² (1,943,945 km²)
Population density: 163 per mi² (63 per km²)

United States of America (USA)
Capital city: Washington, D.C.
Population: 326,625,791
Land area: 3,531,905m² (9,147,593 km²)
Population density: 86 per mi² (33 per km²)

CENTRAL AMERICA

Belize
Capital city: Belmopan
Population: 360,346
Land area: 8,805 mi² (22,806 km²)
Population density: 44 per mi² (17 per km²)

Costa Rica
Capital city: San José
Population: 4,930,258
Land area: 19,714 mi² (51,060 km²)
Population density: 251 per mi² (97 per km²)

El Salvador
Capital city: San Salvador
Population: 6,172,011
Land area: 8,000 mi² (20,721 km²)
Population density: 811 per mi² (313 per km²)

Guatemala
Capital city: Guatemala City
Population: 15,460,732
Land area: 41,374 mi² (107,159 km²)
Population density: 376 per mi² (145 per km²)

Honduras
Capital city: Tegucigalpa
Population: 9,038,741
Land area: 43,201 mi² (111,890 km²)
Population density: 207 per mi² (80 per km²)

Nicaragua
Capital city: Managua
Population: 6,025,951
Land area: 46,328 mi² (119,990 km²)
Population density: 135 per mi² (52 per km²)

Panama
Capital city: Panama City
Population: 3,753,142
Land area: 28,703 per mi² (74,340 km²)
Population density: 145 per mi² (56 per km²)

UNITED STATES OF AMERICA

Los Angeles, California, is the city with the second-highest population in the United States. New York City has the highest.

Mexico is a prime producer of crude oil and natural gas, but output is decreasing.

MEXICO

Guatemala's ancient Mayan civilization is evident in the cities they built 8,000 years ago.

GUATEMALA

BELIZE

EL SALVADOR

HONDURAS

Fact
Eighty percent of Central American forests have been turned over to agriculture and grazing, leaving 300 species of **flora** and **fauna** threatened.

GREENLAND
(Denmark)

Baffin Bay

Nuuk

Iqaluit

Labrador Sea

Hudson Bay

D A

Lake Winnipeg

Winnipeg

Lake Superior

Québec City

Ottawa

Montreal

St. John

Halifax

Lake Huron

Toronto

ke toba

Paul

Lake Michigan

Detroit

New York City

Boston

Lake Ontario

Philadelphia

T A T E S

Chicago

Lake Erie

sas City

Indianapolis

Cincinnati

Washington D.C.

R I C A

Nashville

lahoma City

Memphis

Atlanta

Dallas

New Orleans

uston

Miami

Gulf of Mexico

Yucatan Peninsula

Mérida

Bay of Campeche

BELIZE
Belmopan

HONDURAS
Tegucigalpa

NICARAGUA
Managua

hmus of uantepec

Panama Canal

UATEMALA
uatemala City

Lake Nicaragua

EL SALVADOR
San Salvador

PANAMA
Panama City

COSTA RICA
San José

NICARAGUA

THE CARIBBEAN

Caribbean Sea

VENEZUELA

COLOMBIA

GO

ST. PIERRE AND MIQUELON
(France)

ATLANTIC OCEAN

BERMUDA
(UK)

Canada has the most lakes (about two million) of any country in the world.

CANADA

NUMBER OF COUNTRIES
10

The White House in Washington, D.C. is the official residence of the president of the USA.

COSTA RICA

PANAMA

The Panama Canal is a human-made shortcut, linking the Atlantic and Pacific oceans.

Flag facts

Belize
Early industries of woodcutting and boatbuilding are represented by the tree, axe, and oar.

Honduras
The five countries of the original Central American republic are represented by the five blue stars.

Canada
The red maple leaf is the world's most recognized national symbol. It represents the unity of all citizens.

Mexico
The eagle, holding a snake, on a cactus repeats the legend of how the Aztecs chose a site for Mexico City.

Costa Rica
The crest shows the country's two coasts, mountain ranges, and valley. The beans mark its coffee industry.

Nicaragua
Inside the triangle of equality are five volcanoes for the original Central American countries.

El Salvador
El Salvador's date of independence circles a sun under a rainbow of peace. The red hat represents **liberty**.

Panama
Modeled on the flag of the USA, white symbolizes peace; red authority and law; and blue, honesty.

Guatemala
Above the scroll is Guatemala's national symbol—a resplendent quetzal, which symbolizes liberty.

USA
The stars represent the 50 states of America. In 1960, Hawaii joined the Union and became the 50th state.

The Caribbean

Cradled between North, Central, and South America and the Atlantic Ocean lie the 7,000 islands and reefs of the Caribbean. Only 2 percent of these mainly volcanic tropical islands are inhabited. The Caribbean contains 13 independent countries and some foreign territories. The population is mostly **descended** from enslaved Africans who worked the sugar **plantations** from the 1620s until slavery was **abolished** in 1848.

Antigua and Barbuda
Capital city: St. John's
Population: 94,731
Land area: 171 mi² (443 km²)
Population density: 505 per mi²
(195 per km²)

Barbados
Capital city: Bridgetown
Population: 292,336
Land area: 166 mi² (430 km²)
Population density: 1,725 per mi²
(666 per km²)

Cuba
Capital city: Havana
Population: 11,147,407
Land area: 42,402 mi²
(109,820 km²)
Population density: 264 per mi²
(102 per km²)

Dominica
Capital city: Roseau
Population: 73,897
Land area: 290 mi² (751 km²)
Population density: 249 per mi²
(96 per km²)

Dominican Republic
Capital city: Santo Domingo
Population: 10,734,247
Land area: 18,656 mi²
(48,320 km²)
Population density: 554 per mi²
(214 per km²)

Haiti, which lies in a hurricane belt, is a very poor country with high unemployment.

CUBA

THE BAHAMAS

HAITI

THE BAHAMAS
Nassau

UNITED STATES OF AMERICA

Gulf of Mexico

Cuba banned the **import** of new cars until 2011, which is why most cars are 1950s classics.

Straits of Florida

Havana

CUBA

Santiago de Cub

Ocho Rios

CAYMAN ISLANDS
(UK)

JAMAICA
Kingston

Carib

Bay of Campeche

M E X I C O

B E L I Z E

GUATEMALA

HONDURAS

NICARAGUA

P A C I F I C   O C E A N

JAMAICA

Grenada
Capital city: St. George's
Population: 111,724
Land area: 133 mi² (344 km²)
Population density: 777 per mi²
(300 per km²)

Haiti
Capital city: Port-au-Prince
Population: 10,646,714
Land area: 10,641 mi² (27,560 km²)
Population density: 1,064 per mi²
(411 per km²)

Jamaica
Capital city: Kingston
Population: 2,990,561
Land area: 4,182 mi² (10,831 km²)
Population density: 642 per mi²
(248 per km²)

St. Kitts and Nevis
Capital city: Basseterre
Population: 52,715
Land area: 101 mi² (261 km²)
Population density: 497 per mi²
(192 per km²)

St. Lucia
Capital city: Castries
Population: 164,994
Land area: 234 mi² (606 km²)
Population density: 754 per mi²
(291 per km²)

St. Vincent and the Grenadines
Capital city: Kingstown
Population: 102,089
Land area: 150 mi² (389 km²)
Population density: 730 per mi²
(282 per km²)

The Bahamas
Capital city: Nassau
Population: 329,988
Land area: 3,865 mi² (10,010 km²)
Population density: 73 per mi²
(28 per km²)

Trinidad and Tobago
Capital city: Port of Spain
Population: 1,218,208
Land area: 1,980 mi² (5,128 km²)
Population density: 681 mi²
(263 per km²)

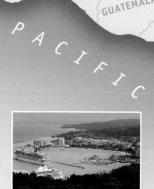

Ocho Rios, Jamaica, with its golden beaches, attracts many tourists. Tourism is very important to the island.

NUMBER OF COUNTRIES
13

Flag facts

Antigua and Barbuda
The rising sun signified a new era when these two islands became self-governing.

Cuba
Communist Cuba's flag was based on the American flag. The white star signifies the path to progress.

Dominican Republic
The Bible on the flag shows this verse: "And the truth shall set you free." (John 8:32)

Jamaica
This is one of only two flags in the world not to use white, red, or blue. Its colors represent sun, strength, and forests.

St. Vincent and the Grenadines
Known as "Jewels of the Caribbean," the diamonds represent this chain of islands.

Barbados
The trident, a three-pronged fork, stands for the principles of government *of*, *for*, and *by* the people.

Dominica
Inside a ring of 10 stars for the parishes on Dominica, sits the sisserou parrot that is **unique** to the island.

Grenada
Nutmeg is so important to this island it is on the flag. The seed sits on green for Grenada's lush vegetation.

St. Kitts and Nevis
The struggle against slavery is signified by the red triangle; sun by the yellow; and hope and liberty by the stars.

Trinidad and Tobago
The red represents the sun and spirit of the people; white, the sea; and black, the land.

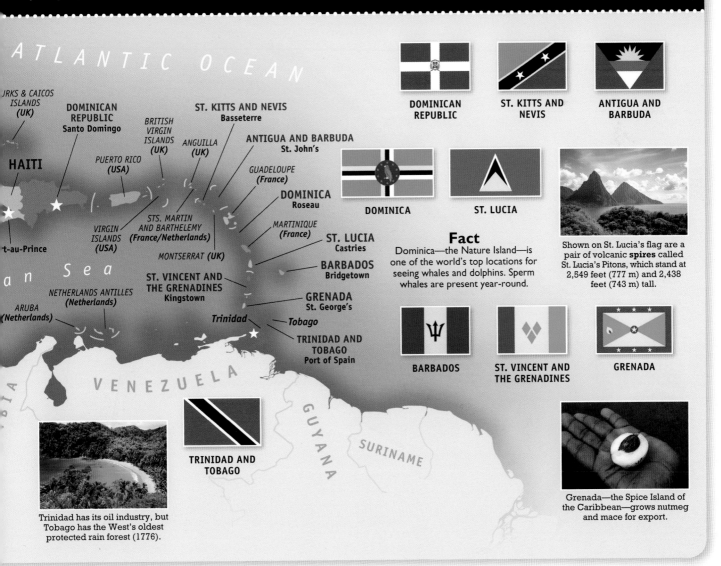

Fact
Dominica—the Nature Island—is one of the world's top locations for seeing whales and dolphins. Sperm whales are present year-round.

Shown on St. Lucia's flag are a pair of volcanic **spires** called St. Lucia's Pitons, which stand at 2,549 feet (777 m) and 2,438 feet (743 m) tall.

Trinidad has its oil industry, but Tobago has the West's oldest protected rain forest (1776).

Grenada—the Spice Island of the Caribbean—grows nutmeg and mace for export.

Northern South America

Surrounded by the Pacific and Atlantic oceans and the Caribbean Sea, this region of seven countries and one French territory boasts the Amazon rain forest, the Andes mountains and the spectacular Angel Falls. The **natural resources** of these countries—oil, gold and gems—were **exploited** by foreign **colonists** for centuries. Despite wealth and self-rule, public services are poor in these seven countries.

Brazil
Capital city: Brasília
Population: 207,353,391
Land area: 3,227,096 mi²
(8,358,140 km²)
Population density:
64 per mi² (25 per km²)

Colombia
Capital city: Bogotá
Population: 47,698,524
Land area: 401,044 mi²
(1,038,700 km²)
Population density:
113 per mi² (44 per km²)

Ecuador
Capital city: Quito
Population: 16,290,913
Land area: 106,889 mi²
(276,841 km²)
Population density:
159 per mi² (61 per km²)

Guyana
Capital city: Georgetown
Population: 737,718
Land area: 76,004 mi²
(196,849 km²)
Population density:
10 per mi² (4 per km²)

Peru
Capital city: Lima
Population: 31,036,656
Land area: 494,209 mi²
(1,279,996 km²)
Population density:
65 per mi² (25 per km²)

Suriname
Capital city: Paramaribo
Population: 591,919
Land mass: 60,232 mi²
(156,000 km²)
Population density:
10 per mi² (4 per km²)

Venezuela
Capital city: Caracas
Population: 31,304,016
Land area: 340,561 mi²
(882,050 km²)
Population density:
83 per mi² (34 per km²)

COLOMBIA

ECUADOR

VENEZUELA

Caribbean Sea

Medellín

Andes

Caracas
VENEZUELA

Bogotá

Angel Falls

Georgetown

Paramaribo

FRENCH GUIANA (France)

GUYANA   SURINAME

Amazon River delta

COLOMBIA

ECUADOR
Quito

GALAPAGOS ISLANDS (Ecuador)

Andes

PACIFIC OCEAN

PERU

Manaus

BRAZIL

Fortaleza

Recife

NUMBER OF COUNTRIES
7

PERU

Lima

Arequipa

BOLIVIA

Lake Titicaca

Salvador

Brasília

Fact
While French Guiana remains a territory of France, Guyana gained its independence from Britain in 1966.

Venezuela has Amazonian jungles, Andean peaks, waterfalls, and golden beaches.

PARAGUAY

Belo Horizonte

São Paulo

Curitiba

Rio de Janeiro

ATLANTIC OCEAN

BRAZIL

SURINAME

Arctic Circle

Tropic of Cancer

North America

The Caribbean

Central America

Equator

Atlantic Ocean

Tropic of Capricorn

Pacific Ocean

South America

Antarctic Circle

Lagoa dos patos

URUGUAY

Suriname's largest community are Asian Indians who follow the Hindu religion.

GUYANA

Brazil is the world's eighth-largest economy, but many millions live in slums (*favelas*).

Flag facts

Brazil
The stars depict the night sky over Rio de Janeiro, Brazil's second-largest city, and stand for Brazil's 27 states.

Ecuador
Atop the crest is an Andean condor, its wings spread to protect the country or to attack an enemy.

Guyana
The colors of the Golden Arrowhead mean (l to r) **spirit**, courage, minerals, waters, and forests.

Suriname
The yellow star signifies the country's unity, its bright future, and the spirit required to achieve progress.

Venezuela
The stars represent the eight provinces that supported Venezuela's fight for independence from Spain 1810–1823.

Southern South America

This region is often referred to as the Southern Cone and is bordered by the Pacific and Atlantic oceans. Ushuaia, at its southerly tip, is so close to the Antarctic it is bitterly cold for much of the year. However, in the north, fertile pampas grasslands are humid and warm. The population of the Southern Cone is chiefly **descendants** of Europeans, who were attracted to the area's natural wealth and almost unlimited land for farming and agriculture.

 Argentina
Capital city: Buenos Aires
Population: 44,293,293
Land area: 1,056,642 mi²
(2,736,690 km²)
Population density:
41 per mi² (16 per km²)

 Bolivia
Capital cities: Sucre and La Paz
Population: 11,138,234
Land area: 418,265 mi²
(1,083,301 km²)
Population density: 26 per mi²
(10 per km²)

Chile
Capital city: Santiago
Population: 17,789,267
Land area: 287,187 mi²
(743,812 km²)
Population density:
60 per mi² (33 per km²)

 Paraguay
Capital city: Asunción
Population: 6,943,739
Land mass: 153,399 mi²
(397,302 km²)
Population density:
44 per mi² (17 per km²)

 Uruguay
Capital city: Montevideo
Population: 3,360,148
Land area: 67,574 mi²
(175,015 km²)
Population density:
52 per mi² (20 per km²)

Flag facts

Argentina
Known as the Sun of May, the face is that of Inti, the Inca god of the Sun and **patron** of the ancient Inca Empire.

Bolivia
The crest shows the country's **natural resources**—rich land and vegetation, alpacas, and wheat.

Chile
White is the snow-capped Andes; blue, the sky; red, the fight for liberty; and the star, a guide to progress.

Paraguay
Unique among flags, the back of Paraguay's flag is different from the front. It shows a lion (peace) and a hat (law).

Uruguay
The nine white and blue bands represent the original regions of Uruguay, and the Sun of May is for liberty.

BOLIVIA

PARAGUAY

CHILE

Santiago's business district is dwarfed by the snow-covered peaks of the Andes.

Fact
The Falkland Islands, off Argentina's coast, are a British overseas territory, though this claim is disputed by Argentina.

 Uruguay generates 95 percent of its electricity from renewables like wind turbines.

NUMBER OF COUNTRIES
5

URUGUAY

ARGENTINA

Buenos Aires' *Avenida 9 de Julio*, celebrates the country's independence and its future.

Northern and Eastern Africa

Northern Africa is bordered on three sides by water and includes most of the Sahara Desert in the south. Eastern Africa, including the Horn of Africa, are sub-Saharan and edged by the Indian Ocean and split by the Great Rift Valley. Northern Africa is home to Berber, Arab, and African people; Eastern Africa has 160 **ethnic** groups. Farming **dominated** the economies of these areas until natural resources, such as oil, were exploited.

NORTHERN AFRICA

Algeria
Capital city: Algiers
Population: 40,969,443
Land area: 919,595 mi² (2,381,741 km²)
Population density: 47 per mi² (18 per km²)

Egypt
Capital city: Cairo
Population: 97,041,072
Land area: 384,345 mi² (995,450 km²)
Population density: 251 per mi² (97 per km²)

Libya
Capital city: Tripoli
Population: 6,653,210
Land area: 679,362 mi² (1,759,540 km²)
Population density: 10 per mi² (4 per km²)

Morocco
Capital city: Rabat
Population: 33,986,655
Land area: 172,317 mi² (446,300 km²)
Population density: 201 per mi² (78 per km²)

South Sudan
Capital city: Juba
Population: 13,026,129
Land area: 238,997 mi² (619,000 km²)
Population density: 52 per mi² (20 per km²)

Sudan
Capital city: Khartoum
Population: 37,345,935
Land area: 718,723 mi² (1,861,484 km²)
Population density: 59 per mi² (22 per km²)

Tunisia
Capital city: Tunis
Population: 11,403,800
Land area: 59,985 mi² (155,360 km²)
Population density: 181 per mi² (70 per km²)

HORN OF AFRICA

Djibouti
Capital city: Djibouti
Population: 865,267
Land area: 8,950 mi² (23,180 km²)
Population density: 98 per mi² (38 per km²)

Eritrea
Capital city: Asmara
Population: 5,918,919
Land area: 38,996 mi² (101,000 km²)
Population density: 117 per mi² (45 per km²)

Ethiopia
Capital city: Addis Ababa
Population: 105,350,020
Land area: 386,102 mi² (1,000,000 km²)
Population density: 249 per mi² (96 per km²)

Somalia
Capital city: Mogadishu
Population: 11,031,386
Land area: 242,216 mi² (627,337 km²)
Population density: 60 per mi² (23 per km²)

MOROCCO

ALGERIA

TUNISIA

LIBYA

Berbers are Northern Africa's original inhabitants. Some still live a traditional **nomadic** life.

Fact
In the scramble for fertile land in the 1800s, almost every corner of Africa was **colonized** by a European power.

Zambia's copper mines support the economy, but low prices have affected public services.

Flag facts

Burundi
Each star represents an ethnic group—Hutu, Tutsi, or Twa—and the goals of work, unity, and progress.

Eritrea
The colors are those of Ethiopia's liberation party. The olive branch inside the wreath signifies peace.

Kenya
The Masai shield and spears represent the fight for freedom and the protection of the people and the land.

Mauritius
The red signifies the battle for liberty; blue, the Indian Ocean; yellow, the light of liberty; green, the land.

Tunisia
The crescent and star are Islamic symbols for harmony, and the star's points represent the five rituals of the faith.

Comoros
The four stripes and stars are Comoros's main islands. The green represents the prophet Muhammad.

Ethiopia
The colors are said to represent the rainbow that appeared after the great flood, according to the book of Genesis.

Malawi
Black, red, and green are the colors of black liberation, and the sun represents the dawn of freedom.

Mozambique
The only flag to depict a modern weapon—an AK 47. Many want it removed, but the ruling party have refused.

Zimbabwe
Soapstone-carved bird sculptures were found in a 1,000-year-old ruin. They became the country's symbol.

TUNISIA
Tunis

NUMBER OF COUNTRIES
24

Mediterranean Sea

EGYPT

Nile delta

Egypt's Bibliotheca Alexandrina has a copy of every web page published since 1996.

Tripoli

Alexandria

Suez Canal

Cairo

LIBYA

esert

EGYPT

Lake Nasser

Somalia has been war-torn since 1991. Millions of Somalis now live in refugee camps.

Port Sudan

Red Sea

SUDAN

ERITREA
Asmara

Khartoum

Ethiopian Highlands

YEMEN

DJIBOUTI
Djibouti

SUDAN

Great Rift Valley

Addis Ababa

Horn of Africa

ERITREA

SOUTH SUDAN

SOUTH SUDAN

ETHIOPIA

SOMALIA

Juba

ETHIOPIA

UGANDA

Lake Turkana

Mogadishu

UGANDA

Kampala

KENYA

KENYA

RWANDA
Kigali

Nairobi

BURUNDI
Bujumbura

Mombasa

Lake Victoria

RWANDA

SOMALIA

DJIBOUTI

TANZANIA

Lake Tanganyika

Dodoma

Dar es Salaam

COMOROS
Moroni

SEYCHELLES
Victoria

BURUNDI

Lake Nyasa (Lake Malawi)

SEYCHELLES

TANZANIA

MALAWI
Lilongwe

INDIAN OCEAN

ZAMBIA

Mozambique Channel

MAYOTTE (France)

MAURITIUS
Port Louis

Lusaka

MADAGASCAR

Harare

Lake Kariba

ZIMBABWE

RÉUNION (France)

ZAMBIA

MOZAMBIQUE

Antananarivo

Maputo

ZIMBABWE

MADAGASCAR

MAURITIUS

COMOROS

MOZAMBIQUE

MALAWI

Burundi
Capital city: Bujumbura
Population: 11,466,756
Land area: 9,915 m² (25,680 km²)
Population density:
995 per mi² (384 per km²)

Comoros
Capital city: Moroni
Population: 808,080
Land area: 863 mi² (2,235 km²)
Population density:
1,121 per mi² (433 per km²)

Kenya
Capital city: Nairobi
Population: 47,615,739
Land area: 219,746 mi²
(569,140 km²)
Population density:
228 per mi² (88 per km²)

Madagascar
Capital city: Antananarivo
Population: 25,054,161
Land area: 224,534 mi² (581,540 km²)
Population density:
114 per mi² (44 per km²)

Malawi
Capital city: Lilongwe
Population: 19,196,246
Land area: 32,324 mi² (94,080 km²)
Population density:
407 per mi² (157 per km²)

Mauritius
Capital city: Port Louis
Population: 1,356,388
Land area: 784 mi² (2,030 km²)
Population density:
1,606 per mi² (620 per km²)

Mozambique
Capital city: Maputo
Population: 26,573,706
Land area: 7 303,623 mi² (86,380 km²)
Population density:
88 per mi² (34 per km²)

Rwanda
Capital city: Kigali
Population: 11,901,484
Land area: 9,524 mi² (24,668 km²)
Population density:
1,181 per mi² (456 per km²)

Seychelles
Capital city: Victoria
Population: 93,920
Land area: 176 mi² (455 km²)
Population density:
546 per mi² (211 per km²)

Tanzania
Capital cities: Dodoma, Dar es Salaam
Population: 53,950,935
Land area: 342,009 mi² (885,800 km²)
Population density:
155 per mi² (60 per km²)

Uganda
Capital city: Kampala
Population: 39,570,125
Land area: 76,101 mi² (197,100 km²)
Population density:
404 per mi² (156 per km²)

Zambia
Capital city: Lusaka
Population: 15,972,000
Land area: 287,028 mi² (743,398 km²)
Population density:
57 per mi² (22 per km²)

Zimbabwe
Capital city: Harare
Population: 13,805,084
Land area: 149,362 mi² (386,847 km²)
Population density:
96 per mi² (37 per km²)

Madagascar's long isolation gave rise to many unique animals, such as the sifaka.

Arctic Circle

Europe

Middle East

Tropic of Cancer

Atlantic Ocean

Equator

Africa

Indian Ocean

Tropic of Capricorn

Madagascar

Antarctic Circle

13

Western Africa

Northern areas of this region are semiarid with low rainfall, but Conakry, Guinea, in the south is the wettest capital city in the world. Though the region is rich in minerals, such as diamonds, most people are poor. Up to 85 percent of Liberians live below the poverty line. In some West African countries, the 2014 outbreak of Ebola, a virus caused by contact with infected animals such as monkeys, caused more than 11,000 deaths.

NUMBER OF COUNTRIES
16

CAPE VERDE

CANARY ISLANDS *(Spain)*

WESTERN SAHARA *(Disputed territory)*

MALI

Mali's Great Mosque of Djenné is the largest sun-dried mud brick building in the world.

ALGERIA

Sahara De

SENEGAL

MAURITANIA

MAURITANIA

Nouakchott

MALI

NIGER

Sahel Desert

Timbuktu

THE GAMBIA

CAPE VERDE
Praia

Dakar

SENEGAL

Gambia River

Great Mosque of Djenné

Bamako

Niamey

Lake Chad

BURKINA FASO

Ouagadougou

GUINEA-BISSAU

THE GAMBIA
Banjul

GUINEA-BISSAU
Bissau

GUINEA

BENIN

TOGO

NIGERIA

Abuja

Porto-Novo

Lagos

Conakry

COTE D'IVOIRE

Lake Volta

Freetown

SIERRA LEONE

Monrovia

Yamoussoukro

Lake Nokoue

Niger delta

CAMEROON

Senegalese workers separating peanuts from the plants. Peanuts are exported around the world.

LIBERIA

Accra

GHANA

Lomé

Gulf of Guinea

ATLANTIC OCEAN

SÃO TOMÉ AND PRINCIPE

GUINEA

SIERRA LEONE

BURKINA FASO

LIBERIA

TOGO

BENIN

GHANA

Guinea has half the world's known bauxite. Red bauxite is a source of aluminum.

COTE D'IVOIRE

Fact
Lake Volta, Ghana, is the world's largest human-made lake. It is 250 miles (400 km) long. More than 77,000 people were relocated when the river was dammed.

Elmina Castle, Ghana, was a 15th-century Portuguese fort. Initially for trading gold, it became a slave-trading post.

PORTUGAL

SPAIN

ITA

MOROCCO

Benin
Capital city: Porto-Novo
Population: 11,038,805
Land area: 42,711 mi²
(110,622 km²)
Population density:
254 per mi² (98 per km²)

Mali
Capital city: Bamako
Population: 17,885,245
Land area: 471,118 mi²
(1,220,190 km²)
Population density:
39 per mi² (15 per km²)

Burkina Faso
Capital city: Ouagadougou
Population: 20,107,509
Land area: 105,715 mi²
(273,800 km²)
Population density:
189 per mi² (73 per km²)

Mauritania
Capital city: Nouakchott
Population: 3,758,571
Land area: 397,955 mi²
(1,030,700 km²)
Population density:
10 per mi² (4 per km²)

Cape Verde
Capital city: Praia
Population: 560,899
Land area: 1,557 mi²
(4,033 km²)
Population density:
344 per mi² (133 per km²)

Niger
Capital city: Niamey
Population: 19,245,344
Land area: 489,076 per mi²
(1,266,700 km²)
Population density:
47 per mi² (18 per km²)

Cote d'Ivoire
Capital city: Yamoussoukro
Population: 24,184,810
Land area: 122,782 m²
(318,003 km²)
Population density:
194 per mi² (75 per km²)

Nigeria
Capital city: Abuja
Population: 190,632,261
Land area: 351,649 mi²
(910,768 km²)
Population density:
549 per mi² (212 per km²)

Ghana
Capital city: Accra
Population: 27,499,924
Land area: 87,851 mi²
(227,533 km²)
Population density:
313 per mi² (121 per km²)

Senegal
Capital city: Dakar
Population: 14,668,522
Land area: 74,336 mi²
(192,530 km²)
Population density:
202 per mi² (78 per km²)

Guinea
Capital city: Conakry
Population: 12,413,867
Land area: 94,872 mi²
(245,717 km²)
Population density:
135 per mi² (52 per km²)

Sierra Leone
Capital city: Freetown
Population: 6,163,195
Land area: 27,653 mi²
(71,620 km²)
Population density:
256 per mi² (99 per km²)

Guinea-Bissau
Capital city: Bissau
Population: 1,792,338
Land area: 10,857 mi²
(28,120 km²)
Population density:
111 per mi² (43 per km²)

The Gambia
Capital city: Banjul
Population: 2,051,363
Land area: 3,907 mi²
(10,120 km²)
Population density:
523 per mi² (202 per km²)

Liberia
Capital city: Monrovia
Population: 4,689,021
Land area: 37,189 mi²
(96,320 km²)
Population density:
114 per mi² (44 per km²)

Togo
Capital city: Lomé
Population: 7,965,055
Land area: 20,998 mi²
(54,385 km²)
Population density:
329 per mi² (127 per km²)

NIGER

r   t

NIGERIA

Benin's Ganvie is a 500-year-old village of 20,000 people built on stilts in Lake Nokoue.

Lagos, Nigeria, has the world's second-largest film industry, producing 200 movies a month.

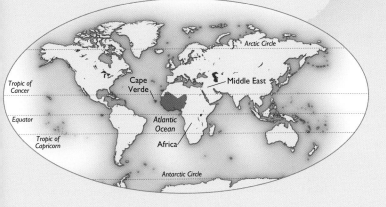

Flag facts

Burkina Faso
The yellow star represents the 1983 revolution that installed a Marxist government in the country.

Mauritania
The Islamic star and the crescent represent the Sahara. Most of this country is desert or semidesert.

Cape Verde
Blue is this country's Atlantic Ocean coast; the red stripe, the road to progress; and the 10 stars, the 10 islands.

Niger
The disk is the sun that shines on Niger's land —represented by green—along the fertile Niger River.

Ghana
Red is the struggle for independence; gold, mineral wealth; green, the rich forests; the star, the lodestar of African freedom.

Sierra Leone
The green, white, and blue represent the country's natural resources, justice, and Freetown's harbor.

Guinea-Bissau
The star represents the unity of African peoples and the red, the sacrifices made for independence.

The Gambia
Red is Gambia's grasslands; blue, the Gambia River; green, the forests; and white, peace.

Liberia
The 11 **signatories** of Liberia's Declaration of Independence are celebrated by the 11 red and white stripes.

Togo
The white "Star of Hope" on a field of red symbolizes the lives lost during Togo's war for independence.

editerranean Sea

A

CHAD

Arctic Circle
Tropic of Cancer
Cape Verde
Middle East
Equator
Atlantic Ocean
Africa
Tropic of Capricorn
Antarctic Circle

Central Africa

The Equator runs across Central Africa while the Congo River—second only to the Amazon in water flow—cuts the region diagonally. The islands of São Tomé and Príncipe lie in the Atlantic Ocean. About 40 percent of the rural population live with food shortages, and oil revenues benefit only a minority. Conflicts in countries such as the Central African Republic have resulted in many deaths and left millions of people needing aid.

Angola
Capital city: Luanda
Population: 29,310,273
Land area: 481,354 mi² (1,246,700 km²)
Population density: 60 per mi² (23 per km²)

Chad
Capital city: N'Djamena
Population: 12,075,985
Land area: 486,180 mi² (1,259,200 km²)
Population density: 31 per mi² (12 per km²)

Cameroon
Capital city: Yaoundé
Population: 24,994,885
Land area: 182,514 mi² (472,710 km²)
Population density: 132 per mi² (51 per km²)

Democratic Republic of the Congo
Capital city: Kinshasa
Population: 83,301,151
Land area: 875,312 mi² (2,267,048 km²)
Population density: 93 per mi² (36 per km²)

Central African Republic
Capital city: Bangui
Population: 5,625,118
Land area: 240,535 mi² (622,984 km²)
Population density: 18 per mi² (7 per km²)

Equatorial Guinea
Capital city: Malabo
Population: 778,358
Land area: 10,831 mi² (28,051 km²)
Population density: 114 per mi² (44 per km²)

Gabon
Capital city: Libreville
Population: 1,772,255
Land area: 99,486 mi² (257,667 km²)
Population density: 21 per mi² (8 per km²)

Republic of the Congo
Capital city: Brazzaville
Population: 4,954,674
Land area: 131,854 mi² (341,500 km²)
Population density: 39 per mi² (15 per km²)

São Tomé and Príncipe
Capital city: São Tomé
Population: 201,025
Land area: 372 mi² (964 km²)
Population density: 563 per mi² (218 per km²)

Many children in Cameroon attend school, then go to work in the fields.

Gabon masks, carved from wood, are celebrated. They represent an ancestor's soul.

NUMBER OF COUNTRIES 9

CAMEROON

EQUATORIAL GUINEA

SÃO TOMÉ AND PRÍNCIPE

GABON

CHAD

REPUBLIC OF THE CONGO

CENTRAL AFRICAN REPUBLIC

LIBYA
NIGER
CHAD
Lake Chad
N'Djamena
NIGERIA
CAMEROON
CENTRAL AFRICAN REPUBLIC
Bangui
EQUATORIAL GUINEA
Malabo
Príncipe
Yaoundé
Congo Basin
REPUBLIC OF THE CONGO
Lake Victoria
SÃO TOMÉ AND PRÍNCIPE
São Tomé
São Tomé
GABON
Brazzaville
DEMOCRATIC REPUBLIC OF CONGO
Great Rift Valley
Libreville
Kinshasa
Lake Tanganyika
ANGOLA
Grand Inga Dam
Kolwezi copper mines
Luanda
ANGOLA
NAMIBIA

Arctic Circle
Tropic of Cancer
Atlantic Ocean
Equator
Africa
Gulf of Guinea
Tropic of Capricorn
Antarctic Circle
ATLANTIC OCEAN

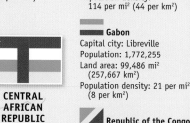
D.R. Congo is home to populations of critically endangered mountain gorillas.

DEMOCRATIC REPUBLIC OF THE CONGO

ANGOLA

Fact
The Grand Inga Dam (Congo River, D.R. Congo) will become the world's largest generator of hydroelectric power.

Flag facts

Angola
The cog represents industrial workers, and the machete, the armed fight of the peasants for freedom.

Chad
Chad's flag is identical to Romania's, a country in Western Europe. Neither country will give up their flag.

Democratic Republic of the Congo
The star—a light in a "dark continent"—marks liberty.

Equatorial Guinea
The coat of arms is a silk cotton tree, or god tree, under which a treaty was signed by a local ruler and Spain.

Republic of the Congo
This is one of seven African countries to use green, yellow, and red on their flag.

Southern Africa

This region has deserts, grasslands, forests, mountains, and plains. It has Indian and Atlantic ocean coasts, but three of its countries are **landlocked**. Political **instability** and **drought** mean that only one Southern African country—South Africa—can feed its population without food aid and reliance on imports. The change from being ruled by Europe to being independent resulted in much violence in this region during mid to late 1900s.

Botswana
Capital city: Gaborone
Population: 2,214,858
Land area: 218,816 mi² (566,730 km²)
Population density: 10 per mi² (4 per km²)

Lesotho
Capital city: Maseru
Population: 1,958,042
Land area: 11,720 mi² (30,355 km²)
Population density: 192 per mi² (74 per km²)

Namibia
Capital city: Windhoek
Population: 2,484,780
Land area: 317,874 mi² (823,290 km²)
Population density: 8 per mi² (3 per km²)

South Africa
Capital cities: Pretoria (Tshwane), Cape Town, Bloemfontein
Population: 54,841,552
Land area: 468,909 mi² (1,214,470 km²)
Population density: 119 per mi² (46 per km²)

Swaziland
Capital cities: Mbabane and Lobamba
Population: 1,467,152
Land area: 6,643 mi² (17,204 km²)
Population density: 171 per mi² (66 per km²)

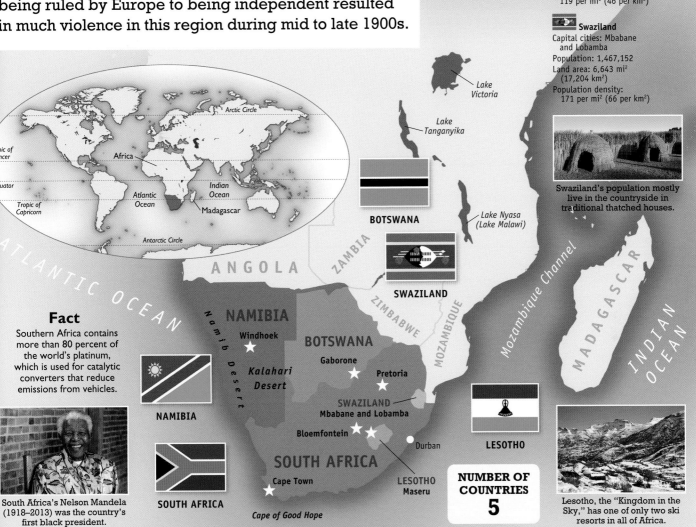

Fact
Southern Africa contains more than 80 percent of the world's platinum, which is used for catalytic converters that reduce emissions from vehicles.

South Africa's Nelson Mandela (1918–2013) was the country's first black president.

Swaziland's population mostly live in the countryside in traditional thatched houses.

NUMBER OF COUNTRIES
5

Lesotho, the "Kingdom in the Sky," has one of only two ski resorts in all of Africa.

Flag Facts

Botswana
The black and white stripes are inspired by the national animal, the zebra, and represent harmony between all.

Lesotho
At the center is a straw Basotho hat. The hat's conical shape was inspired by Mount Qiloane, Lesotho.

Namibia
The 12-rayed sun, symbolizing power, sits on a background representing sky, rain, and water.

South Africa
The Y-shape shows different races coming together in unity and harmony in a post-**apartheid** South Africa.

Swaziland
The shield, spears, and staff represent protection, while the black and white speaks of unity between races.

Northern Europe and Russia

Bordered by oceans or seas and ranging from temperate to subarctic, Northern Europe and Russia have fertile uplands and plains, mineral wealth, strong industries, and highly developed communications. Finland, Denmark, Sweden, Norway, and Iceland are known as Nordic countries, and some are in the top 10 of countries with high standards of living. Though most of Russia lies in Asia, most of its population is European.

Sweden recycles 99 percent of its trash. The energy produced is used to heat homes.

SWEDEN

Norway has about 1,190 fjords. A fjord is a deep narrow inlet of seawater between high cliffs.

ICELAND
Reykjavik

ICELAND

Iceland has more than 20 active volcanoes. The largest volcano covers 8 percent of the island.

United Kingdom has Europe's highest percentage (1 in 10) of mixed-raced families.

UNITED KINGDOM

IRELAND

NORWAY

DENMARK

LATVIA

ESTONIA

LITHUANIA

Fact
Ireland's national language is Irish, but the dominant language is English. Polish is the second most widely spoken language there.

Denmark
Capital city: Copenhagen
Population: 5,605,948
Land area: 16,384 mi² (42,434 km²)
Population density: 347 per mi² (134 per km²)

Finland
Capital city: Helsinki
Population: 5,518,371
Land area: 117,304 mi² (303,815 km²)
Population density: 41 per mi² (16 per km²)

Ireland
Capital city: Dublin
Population: 5,011,102
Land area: 26,596 mi² (68,883 km²)
Population density: 176 per mi² (68 per km²)

Estonia
Capital city: Tallinn
Population: 1,251,581
Land area: 16,366 mi² (42,388 km²)
Population density: 75 per mi² (29 per km²)

Iceland
Capital city: Reykjavik
Population: 339,747
Land area: 38,707 mi² (100,250 km²)
Population density: 9 per mi² (3.5 per km²)

Latvia
Capital city: Riga
Population: 1,944,643
Land area: 24,034 mi² (62,249 km²)
Population density: 89 per mi² (34 per km²)

Flag facts

Denmark
The Danneberg is the world's oldest flag. During a battle in 1219, this flag is said to have fallen from the sky.

Latvia
The red is the blood of a wounded Latvian leader, and the white, the cloth used to wrap his wounds.

Estonia
Blue is the skies and waters; black, the fertile soil; and white, the winter snow.

Lithuania
The yellow represents the fields of wheat; green, the forests; and red, patriotism and the courage of the people.

Finland
The blue Scandinavian cross stands for the country's lakes, and the white is the snow that covers the land.

Russian Federation
White is nobility; blue, loyalty and honesty; and red, courage, generosity, and love.

Iceland
The flag describes the landscape: blue, the Atlantic Ocean; red, volcanoes; and white, snow and ice.

Sweden
The cross echoes the legend that Eric the Holy, a 12th-century king, saw a golden cross in the sky.

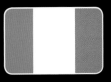

Ireland
The orange represents Ireland's Protestants; green, the Catholics; and white, the truce between them.

United Kingdom
This flag combines the crosses of England's St. George, Scotland's St. Andrew, and Ireland's St. Patrick.

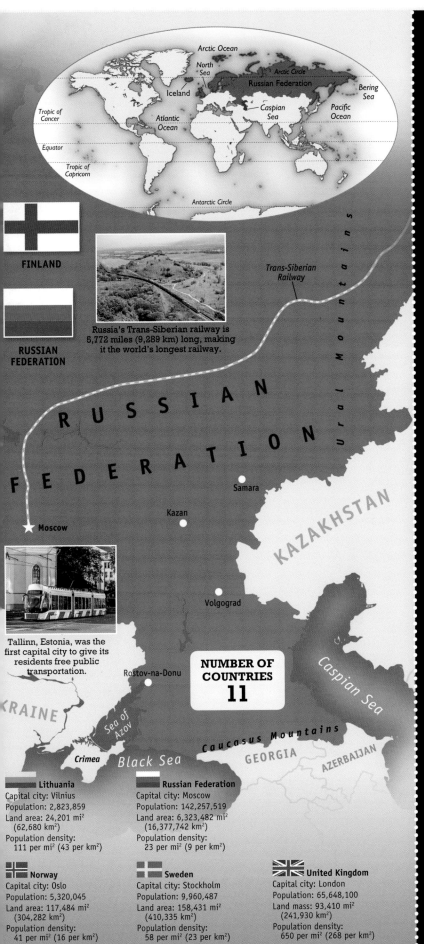

FINLAND

RUSSIAN FEDERATION

Russia's Trans-Siberian railway is 5,772 miles (9,289 km) long, making it the world's longest railway.

Trans-Siberian Railway

Tallinn, Estonia, was the first capital city to give its residents free public transportation.

NUMBER OF COUNTRIES
11

Lithuania
Capital city: Vilnius
Population: 2,823,859
Land area: 24,201 mi² (62,680 km²)
Population density: 111 per mi² (43 per km²)

Russian Federation
Capital city: Moscow
Population: 142,257,519
Land area: 6,323,482 mi² (16,377,742 km²)
Population density: 23 per mi² (9 per km²)

Norway
Capital city: Oslo
Population: 5,320,045
Land area: 117,484 mi² (304,282 km²)
Population density: 41 per mi² (16 per km²)

Sweden
Capital city: Stockholm
Population: 9,960,487
Land area: 158,431 mi² (410,335 km²)
Population density: 58 per mi² (23 per km²)

United Kingdom
Capital city: London
Population: 65,648,100
Land mass: 93,410 mi² (241,930 km²)
Population density: 650 per mi² (268 per km²)

Western Europe

The countries of Western Europe combine industrial development, commercial agriculture, technological innovation, and an educated and skilled labor force to create high standards of living. Luxembourg is the second-richest country in the world. In the 1900s, this region and beyond was war torn. To encourage unity after World War Two, the foundations of what would become the European Union were laid.

The Netherlands is very flat and more than a quarter of the land is below sea level.

Luxembourg was one of the most fortified cities in Europe. It is a World Heritage Site.

NETHERLANDS

GERMANY

AUSTRIA

BELGIUM

FRANCE

MONACO

LIECHTENSTEIN

SWITZERLAND

Fact
Switzerland is the oldest neutral country in the world. It has not fought in a foreign war since 1815.

NUMBER OF COUNTRIES
9

France is the world's largest consumer of electricity generated by nuclear fuels.

Austria
Capital city: Vienna
Population: 8,754,413
Land area: 31,832 mi² (82,445 km²)
Population density:
272 per mi² (105 per km²)

Belgium
Capital city: Brussels
Population: 11,491,346
Land area: 11,690 mi² (30,278 km²)
Population density:
969 per mi² (374 per km²)

France
Capital city: Paris
Population: 62,814,233*
Land area: 212,345 mi²
(549,970 km²)*
Population density:
321 per mi² (124 per km²)*

Germany
Capital city: Berlin
Population: 80,594,017
Land area: 134,623 mi²
(348,672 km²)
Population density:
598 per mi² (231 per km²)

Liechtenstein
Capital city: Vaduz
Population: 38,244
Land area: 62 mi² (160 km²)
Population density:
614 per mi² (237 per km²)

Luxembourg
Capital city: Luxembourg
Population: 594,130
Land area: 998 mi² (2,586 km²)
Population density:
603 per mi² (233 per km²)

Monaco
Capital city: Monaco
Population: 30,645
Land area: 0.77 mi² (2 km²)
Population density:
48,145 per mi² (18,598 per km²)

Netherlands
Capital city: Amsterdam
Population: 17,084,719
Land area: 13,086 mi² (33,893 km²)
Population density:
1,074 per mi² (415 per km²)

Switzerland
Capital city: Bern
Population: 8,236,303
Land area: 195 per mi² (39,997 km²)
Population density:
531 per mi² (205 per km²)

* (excluding territories)

Eastern Europe

Running diagonally across Europe from the Baltic Sea to the Black Sea, the plains of this region are split by the Carpathian Mountains. Eastern Europe's nine **diverse** countries are bound together by having been behind the Soviet Union's fortified **Iron Curtain** from 1945 to 1989. This left their economies in a poor state. Today, agriculture thrives along with manufacturing and industry; coal, oil, and natural gas mining; and tourism.

Belarus
Capital city: Minsk
Population: 9,549,747
Land area: 78,340 mi² (202,900 km²)
Population density: 119 per mi² (46 per km²)

Bulgaria
Capital city: Sofia
Population: 7,101,510
Land area: 41,888 mi² (108,489 km²)
Population density: 166 per mi² (64 per km²)

Czechia (Czech Republic)
Capital city: Prague
Population: 10,674,723
Land area: 29,825 mi² (77,247 km²)
Population density: 350 per mi² (135 per km²)

Hungary
Capital city: Budapest
Population: 9,850,845
Land area: 34,598 mi² (89,608 km²)
Population density: 272 per mi² (105 per km²)

Moldova
Capital city: Chisinau
Population: 3,474,121
Land area: 12,699 mi² (32,891 km²)
Population density: 272 per mi² (105 per km²)

Poland
Capital city: Warsaw
Population: 38,476,269
Land area: 117,474 mi² (304,255 km²)
Population density: 319 per mi² (123 per km²)

Romania
Capital city: Bucharest
Population: 21,529,967
Land area: 88,761 mi² (229,891 km²)
Population density: 212 per mi² (82 per km²)

Slovakia
Capital city: Bratislava
Population: 5,445,829
Land area: 18,573 mi² (48,105 km²)
Population density: 287 per mi² (111 per km²)

Ukraine
Capital city: Kyiv
Population: 44,033,874
Land area: 223,681 mi² (579,330 km²)
Population density: 181 per mi² (70 per km²)

Auschwitz, Poland, where 1.5 million Jews and Poles were killed during World War Two.

POLAND

CZECHIA (CZECH REPUBLIC)

SLOVAKIA

Hungary is rich in thermal waters and there are 150 hot water spas in the country.

HUNGARY

Plovdiv, Bulgaria, is Europe's oldest inhabited city with neolithic and ancient sites.

BULGARIA

ROMANIA

NUMBER OF COUNTRIES
9

Fact
Poland, Bulgaria, and Romania are the three poorest countries in the European Union.

LITHUANIA
Baltic Sea
RUSSIAN FEDERATION
Minsk
BELARUS
POLAND
GERMANY
Warsaw
Łódz
Auschwitz
Kraków
Prague
CZECHIA (CZECH REPUBLIC)
SLOVAKIA
Bratislava
HUNGARY
Budapest
CROATIA
SERBIA
Carpathian Mountains
Kyiv (Kiev)
UKRAINE
MOLDOVA
Chisinau
Odessa
Crimea
Donetsk
Sea of Azov
ROMANIA
Bucharest
BULGARIA
Plovdiv
Sofia
Black Sea

UKRAINE

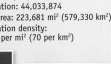
BELARUS

MOLDOVA

Arctic Circle
Atlantic Ocean
Eastern Europe
Tropic of Cancer
Equator
Tropic of Capricorn
Antarctic Circle

Flag facts

Belarus
The decorative pattern is a traditional embroidery that is found on peasant shirts and blouses.

Czechia (Czech Republic)
Derived from the Bohemian coat of arms, the flag colors symbolize peace, truth, and courage.

Moldova
The eagle holds an Orthodox cross in its beak and an auroch, an extinct European ox, appears on the shield.

Slovakia
Below the double cross are three symbolic peaks—Matra, Fatra, and Tatra. Matra lies inside Hungary.

Ukraine
Once the colors of a coat of arms, the blue and yellow now represent skies over fields of golden wheat.

Southern Europe

The coasts of this region stretch along the Atlantic Ocean and the Mediterranean Sea, and end where "East meets West." The climate is broadly similar end-to-end—warm summers and mild winters. As happened in Eastern Europe, many countries here were Soviet states until the end of the **Cold War**. After years of being in the European Union, some countries in Southern Europe are in the midst of **financial crisis**.

**NUMBER OF COUNTRIES
16**

Croatia's Zlatni Rat Beach changes shape and length with the wind and the tide.

SLOVENIA

BOSNIA AND HERZEGOVINA

CROATIA

Albania
Capital city: Tirana
Population: 3,047,987
Land area: 10,578 mi² (27,398 km²)
Population density: 259 per mi² (100 per km²)

Andorra
Capital city: Andorra la Vella
Population: 76,965
Land mass: 181 mi² (468 km²)
Population density: 448 per mi² (173 per km²)

Bosnia and Herzegovina
Capital city: Sarajevo
Population: 3,856,181
Land area: 19,763 mi² (51,187 km²)
Population density: 179 per mi² (69 per km²)

Croatia
Capital city: Zagreb
Population: 4,292,095
Land area: 21,612 mi² (55,974 km²)
Population density: 189 per mi² (73 per km²)

Greece
Capital city: Athens
Population: 10,768,477
Land area: 50,443 mi² (130,647 km²)
Population density: 212 per mi² (82 per km²)

Italy
Capital city: Rome
Population: 62,137,802
Land area: 113,568 mi² (294,140 km²)
Population density: 521 per mi² (201 per km²)

Kosovo
Capital city: Pristina
Population: 1,895,250
Land mass: 4,203 mi² (10,887 km²)
Population density: 422 per mi² (163 per km²)

Macedonia
Capital city: Skopje
Population: 2,103,721
Land area: 9,820 mi² (25,433 km²)
Population density: 210 per mi² (81 per km²)

SPAIN

Spain celebrates many festivals. The most famous is the Running of the Bulls.

Bay of Biscay

Andorra is in the Pyrenees, so it's all mountainous. There are 65 peaks in the tiny country.

ANDORRA

SWITZERLAND

ALPS

Lake Garda

Milan

Turin

SAN MARINO
San Marino

FRANCE

Santiago de Compostela

Bilbao

Pyrenees

Braga
Porto

ANDORRA
Andorra la Vella

Zaragoza

Barcelona

Ligurian Sea

Corsica (France)

Vatican City

SPAIN

Lisbon

★ Madrid

ITALY

Mallorca *Menorca*

Ibiza

Valencia

Balearic Islands

Formentera

Mediterranean Sea

Sardinia (Italy)

Tyrrhen

Cagliari

PORTUGAL

Seville

Gulf of Cadiz

Malaga

Strait of Gibraltar

GIBRALTAR (UK)

CEUTA (Spain)

MELILLA (Spain)

MOROCCO

ALGERIA

Italy has more masterpieces of art per square mile (2.5 km) than any other country.

TUNISIA

PORTUGAL

AZORES (Portugal)

SPAIN

PORTUGAL

MADEIRA (Portugal)

CANARIES (Spain)

Arctic Circle

Atlantic Ocean

Canaries (Spain)

Africa

Tropic of Cancer

Equator

Tropic of Capricorn

Antarctic Circle

VATICAN CITY

Fact
In October 2017, Catalonia in northeastern Spain declared its independence. The Spanish government imposed **direct rule**.

Malta
Capital city: Valletta
Population: 416,338
Land area: 122 mi² (316 km²)
Population density:
  3,784 per mi² (1,461 per km²)

San Marino
Capital city: San Marino
Population: 33,357
Land area: 24 mi² (61 km²)
Population density:
  1,414 per mi² (546 per km²)

Spain
Capital city: Madrid
Population: 48,958,159
Land area: 192,657 mi² (498,980 km²)
Population density:
  238 per mi² (92 per km²)

Montenegro
Capital city: Podgorica
Population: 642,550
Land area: 5,194 mi² (13,452 km²)
Population density:
  117 per mi² (45 per km²)

Serbia
Capital city: Belgrade
Population: 7,111,024
Land area: 29,913 mi² (77,474 km²)
Population density:
  231 per mi² (89 per km²)

Vatican City State
Capital city: Vatican City
Population: 1,000
Land area: 0.17 mi² (0.44 km²)
Population density:
  4,709 per mi² (1,818 per km²)

Portugal
Capital city: Lisbon
Population: 10,839,514
Land area: 35,317 mi² (91,470 km²)
Population density:
  290 per mi² (112 per km²)

Slovenia
Capital city: Ljubljana
Population: 1,972,126
Land area: 7,780 mi² (20,151 km²)
Population density:
  264 per mi² (102 per km²)

MONTENEGRO

SAN MARINO

SERBIA

KOSOVO

ALBANIA

MACEDONIA

GREECE

MALTA

Maltese fishing boats (*luzzu*)
are very colorful. A pair of
eyes painted on the bow
ward off evil spirits.

Greece's high unemployment
and massive debt has
prompted riots and marches.

Albania
Known as the "Land of
the Eagle," the double-
headed eagle is the
emblem of a national
hero, Skanderbeg.

Montenegro
The double-headed
eagle—the unity of
church and state—
is protected by the
Lion of Judah (Christ).

Bosnia
The triangle stands for
the three peoples of
Bosnia—Bosniaks,
Serbs, and Croats—
and the stars, Europe.

Portugal
The golden sphere—
a navigation device—
honors Portugal's
explorers of the 1400s
and their discoveries.

Greece
The stripes represent
the syllables in the
Greek battle cry of
Eleutheria H Thanatos,
"Freedom or Death."

Slovenia
The stars represent
a noble family; the
peaks, the Julian Alps;
and the blue lines,
access to the sea.

Macedonia
The eight-rayed Sun of
Liberty is a stylized
version of an ancient
symbol found on many
Macedonian artifacts.

Spain
The words on the red
bands mean "More
Beyond" and mark
Columbus's claiming
of America for Spain.

Malta
The George cross
celebrates the award
given by King George
VI to honor the bravery
of the Maltese.

Vatican City
The silver key is the
Pope's authority; the
golden key, his faith;
and together, they are
the keys to heaven.

Southwest Asia

The region is surrounded by the Mediterranean, Aegean, Black, Caspian, Red, and Arabian seas and bordered in the north by the Caucasus Mountains. It has deserts, like the Arabian Peninsula's Empty Quarter, and vast areas of fertile land and forest. Water shortage is a common problem. Oil and natural gas are major industries, but this wealth has not always helped to reduce the poverty that exists in many countries.

NUMBER OF COUNTRIES
19

Istanbul, Turkey, has the world's oldest and largest bazaar. It has 3,000 shops.

TURKEY

CYPRUS

In Paphos, Cyprus, is a 2nd-century villa decorated with beautiful Roman **mosaics**.

Mediterranean Se

Armenia
Capital city: Yerevan
Population: 3,045,191
Land area: 10,889 mi² (28,203 km²)
Population density:
259 per mi² (100 per km²)

Azerbaijan
Capital city: Baku
Population: 9,961,396
Land area: 31,903 mi² (82,629 km²)
Population density:
295 per mi² (114 per km²)

Bahrain
Capital city: Manama
Population: 1,410,942
Land area: 293 mi² (760 km²)
Population density:
4,965 per mi² (1,917 per km²)

Cyprus
Capital city: Nicosia
Population: 1,221,549
Land area: 3,568 mi² (9,241 km²)
Population density:
376 per mi² (145 per km²)

Georgia
Capital city: Tbilisi
Population: 4,926,330
Land area: 26,911 mi² (69,700 km²)
Population density:
137 per mi² (53 per km²)

Iran
Capital city: Tehran
Population: 82,021,564
Land area: 591,352 mi² (1,531,595 km²)
Population density:
128 per mi² (49 per km²)

Iraq
Capital city: Baghdad
Population: 39,192,111
Land area: 168,868 mi² (437,367 km²)
Population density:
228 per mi² (88 per km²)

Israel
Capital city: Jerusalem
Population: 8,299,706 (includes Golan and East Jerusalem)
Land area: 7,849 mi² (20,330 km²)
Population density:
1,040 per mi² (402 per km²)

Jordan
Capital city: Amman
Population: 10,248,069
Land area: 34,287 mi² (88,802 km²)
Population density:
295 per mi² (114 per km²)

Kuwait
Capital city: Kuwait City
Population: 2,875,422
Land area: 6,880 mi² (17,818 km²)
Population density:
583 per mi² (225 per km²)

Lebanon
Capital city: Beirut
Population: 6,229,794
Land area: 3,950 mi² (10,230 km²)
Population density: 1,546 per mi² (597 per km²)

Oman
Capital city: Muscat
Population: 4,613,241
Land area: 119,499 mi² (309,500 km²)
Population density:
36 per mi² (14 per km²)

LEBANON

STATE OF PALESTINE

ISRAEL

The Dead Sea, straddling the Jordan–Israel border, is six times saltier than seawater.

JORDAN

Flag facts

Cyprus
Cyprus is one of two flags that depict its land area. The olive branches represent peace and harmony.

Iran
The symbol is a stylized depiction of the word *Allah* (God) and "There is no God but Allah."

Israel
The Star of David is a symbol of Judaism, and the colors are those of the Jewish prayer shawl, called a *tallit*.

Lebanon
The cedar stands for endurance. Cedar forests, once common in Lebanon, are now being regenerated.

Qatar
The nine-pointed stripe represents Qatar as the ninth Arab state to join a treaty from the 1800s with Britain.

Georgia
The four Bolnisi crosses are a national symbol inspired by those in a Georgian church from the 400s.

Iraq
Inspired by a poem, red is a willingness to shed blood; green, fields; black, battles; and white, purity.

Jordan
The star's seven points represent the seven verses said in prayer in the second of the five Pillars of Islam.

Oman
The short, curved dagger, the *Khanjar*, is a national symbol and is worn by men on ceremonial occasions.

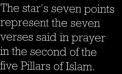
Saudi Arabia
The text is the Muslim oath of faith: "There is no God but Allah." The sword is that of the House of Saud.

GEORGIA

ARMENIA

AZERBAIJAN

Gobustan, Azerbaijan, is known for 6,000 rock engravings that date back 5,000 to 40,000 years.

IRAQ

IRAN

Qatar
Capital city: Doha
Population: 2,314,307
Land area: 4,473 mi² (11,586 km²)
Population density:
603 per mi² (233 per km²)

Saudi Arabia
Capital city: Riyadh
Population: 28,571,770
Land area: 830,000 mi²
(2,149,690 km²)
Population density:
41 per mi² (16 per km²)

State of Palestine
(East Jerusalem, Gaza Strip, West Bank—disputed)
Capital city: East Jerusalem
(disputed)
Population: 5,039,191
Land area: 2,324 mi² (6,020 km²)
Population density:
2,072 per mi² (800 per km²)

Syria
Capital city: Damascus
Population: 18,028,549
Land area: 70,900 mi²
(183,630 km²)
Population density:
256 per mi² (99 per km²)

Turkey
Capital city: Ankara
Population: 80,845,215
Land area: 297,157 mi²
(769,632 km²)
Population density:
267 per mi² (103 per km²)

United Arab Emirates
Capital city: Abu Dhabi
Population: 9,525,176
Land area: 32,278 mi² (83,600 km²)
Population density:
306 per mi² (118 per km²)

Yemen
Capital city: Sanaa
Population: 28,036,829
Land area: 203,850 mi²
(527,968 km²)
Population density:
161 mi² (62 per km²)

RUSSIAN FEDERATION

KAZAKHSTAN

Black Sea

Sea of Marmara

Caucasus Mountains

GEORGIA

Tbilisi

Baku

TURKMENISTAN

Istanbul

Bursa

Ankara

TURKEY

ARMENIA

Yerevan

AZERBAIJAN

Azerbaijan

Caspian Sea

Mashhad

AFGHANISTAN

Aegean Sea

Lake Tuz

Adana

Lake Van

Tabriz

Lake Urmia

CYPRUS
Nicosia

SYRIA

Mosel

Tehran

Therthar Lake

Isfahan

IRAN

LEBANON
Beirut

Damascus

Baghdad

Zagros Mountains

West Bank

IRAQ

Bandar Mahshahr

PAKISTAN

Gaza Strip

Amman

Basra

ISRAEL
Jerusalem

Dead Sea

JORDAN

Persian Gulf

EGYPT

Fact
The Middle East is where Christianity, Judaism, and Islam were born. Jerusalem, Israel, is sacred to all three, but Mecca, Saudi Arabia, is most holy to Islam.

KUWAIT
Kuwait City

Oman

BAHRAIN
Manama

Oman

Dubai

Gulf of Oman

SAUDI
ARABIA

Medina

QATAR
Doha

Abu Dhabi

Muscat

Riyadh

UNITED ARAB
EMIRATES

Sur

Jiddah
(Jeddah)

OMAN

Duqm

Mecca

Red Sea

Empty Quarter

Arabian Sea

SUDAN

Abha

Salalah

SYRIA

ERITREA

Sanaa

YEMEN

SOCOTRA
(Yemen)

UNITED ARAB
EMIRATES

Abu Dhabi is the capital of the United Arab Emirates, which is a federation of seven states.

Al Mukalla

SAUDI ARABIA

KUWAIT

Ta'izz

Aden

Gulf of Aden

SOMALIA

YEMEN

QATAR

Yemen's dragonblood trees have a red sap. It was used by gladiators to heal wounds.

OMAN

BAHRAIN

Arctic Circle

Europe

Asia

Tropic of Cancer

Africa

Equator

Indian Ocean

Tropic of Capricorn

Antarctic Circle

Central Asia

This region's boundaries are broadly set by the Caspian Sea, Hindu Kush mountains, and the borders of China and Russia. The Silk Road—a trade route between China and Europe since 114 B.C.E.—crosses this mostly mountainous area where "East meets West." While Afghanistan, long affected by conflict, is ranked among the world's poorest countries, Kazakhstan with its oil and gas resources is richer than Russia.

Afghanistan
Capital city: Kabul
Population: 34,124,811
Land area: 251,827 mi² (652,230 km²)
Population density:
  119 per mi² (46 per km²)

Kazakhstan
Capital city: Astana
Population: 18,556,698
Land area: 1,042,360 mi² (2,699,700 km²)
Population density:
  18 per mi² (7 per km²)

Kyrgyzstan (Kyrgyz Republic)
Capital city: Bishkek
Population: 5,789,122
Land area: 74,055 mi² (191,801 km²)
Population density:
  81 per mi² (31 per km²)

Tajikistan
Capital city: Dushanbe
Population: 8,468,555
Land area: 54,637 mi²
  (141,510 km²)
Population density:
  161 per mi² (62 per km²)

Turkmenistan
Capital city: Ashgabat
Population: 5,351,277
Land area: 181,441 mi²
  (469,930 km²)
Population density:
  31 per mi² (12 per km²)

Uzbekistan
Capital city: Tashkent
Population: 29,748,859
Land area: 164,248 mi²
  (425,400 km²)
Population density:
  277 per mi² (107 per km²)

KAZAKHSTAN

Kazakhstan's Baikonur Cosmodrome is the world's largest space launch center.

UZBEKISTAN

Uzbekistan has architectural beauty, such as Samarkand's mosque, and mineral wealth.

TURKMENISTAN

KYRGYZSTAN

Fact
These countries' names end with "stan," which means "land of." Afghanistan, for example, is the "land of the Afghan people."

TAJIKISTAN

Tajikistan's Pamir Highway to the "roof of the world" is one of the world's remotest areas.

NUMBER OF COUNTRIES
6

AFGHANISTAN

Map labels: RUSSIAN FEDERATION, Petropavlovsk, Kokshetau, Uralsk, Astana, Lake Zaysan, Lake Alakol, KAZAKHSTAN, Atyrau, Baikonur Cosmodrome, Lake Balkhash, Lake Issyk Kul, Aral Sea, Almaty, Aktau, Caspian Sea, UZBEKISTAN, Tashkent, Bishkek, Jalal-Abad, KYRGYZSTAN, CHINA, Turkmenbashi, Samarkand, TURKMENISTAN, Ashgabat, Turkmenabat, Dushanbe, TAJIKISTAN, Kulob, IRAN, Mazari Sharif, Jalalabad, AFGHANISTAN, Kabul, PAKISTAN, Kandahar, Lashkar-Gah

Globe labels: Arctic Circle, Europe, Russian Federation, China, Tropic of Cancer, Equator, Middle East, Tropic of Capricorn, Antarctic Circle

Flag facts

Afghanistan
The symbol is of a mosque with the arch-topped niche (the *mihrab*) facing Mecca, Islam's holiest site.

Kazakhstan
The blue symbolizes Tengri, god of the sky; and the golden steppe eagle is the country's bright future.

Kyrgyzstan
A yurt—a home used by nomads—is circled by a Sun with 40 rays. Each ray represents a Kyrgyzstan tribe.

Turkmenistan
Five carpet designs appear in the decorative border. Turkmen carpets are a major industry.

Uzbekistan
The new moon is a symbol for Islam and for the birth of a nation. The stars represent the months of the year.

South Asia

South Asia has a fifth of the world's population with Maldives and Bangladesh being in the top 20 of the most densely populated, and India likely to be the most populous country by 2028, overtaking China. Bounded by the Himalayas and the Arabian Sea, Indian Ocean and Bay of Bengal, this region has the economic might of India, but also flood- and cyclone-prone Bangladesh where 24 percent live below the poverty line.

NUMBER OF COUNTRIES
7

Bangladesh
Capital city: Dhaka
Population: 157,826,578
Land area: 50,259 mi²
(130,170 km²)
Population density:
2,961 per mi² (1,143 per km²)

Bhutan
Capital city: Thimphu
Population: 758,288
Land area: 14,824 mi² (38,394 km²)
Population density:
54 per mi² (21 per km²)

India
Capital city: New Delhi
Population: 1,281,935,911
Land area: 1,147,956 mi²
(2,973,193 km²)
Population density:
1,050 per mi² (405 per km²)

Bhutan's government banned mountain climbing in 2004 out of respect for Buddhist beliefs.

BHUTAN   **NEPAL**

BANGLADESH

INDIA

Maldives
Capital city: Malé
Population: 392,709
Land area: 115 mi² (298 km²)
Population density:
3,415 per mi² (1,318 per km²)

Nepal
Capital city: Kathmandu
Population: 29,384,297
Land area: 55,348 mi² (143,351 km²)
Population density:
531 mi² (205 per km²)

Pakistan
Capital city: Islamabad
Population: 204,924,861
Land area: 297,637 mi² (770,875 km²)
Population density:
689 per mi² (266 per km²)

Sri Lanka
Capital city: Colombo
Population: 22,409,381
Land area: 24,954 mi² (64,630 km²)
Population density:
898 per mi² (347 per km²)

Sialkot, Pakistan, has a worldwide reputation for its hand-stitched soccer balls.

SRI LANKA

MALDIVES

India's *Kumbh Mela* is an event in which up to 120 million Hindus bathe in the Ganges River.

Fact
Bangladesh on the Ganges delta floods regularly. The 1988 flood made 30 million homeless and covered 75 percent of the country.

PAKISTAN

Flag facts

Bhutan
Known as the "Land of the Thunder Dragon." The dragon, clutching jewels for wealth, is a national symbol.

India
This flag, by law, has to be made of *Khadi*, a hand-spun cloth that was made popular by Mahatma Gandhi.

Nepal
Unique in its shape—two joined triangles—the symbols signify that Nepal will last as long as the Sun and Moon.

Pakistan
The white stripe represents the minority religions; green, the majority Islam religion; and the star, light.

Sri Lanka
The lion and sword represent authority; green, the Muslim religion; and orange, the Buddhist religion.

East Asia

This region is only 15 percent larger than Europe, but it is one of the most populous places on Earth. Mongolia is the exception in that its population density is very low. China and Japan are top-five world economies, and South Korea is a technology leader. East Asia's climate and rainfall support agriculture, especially growing rice. Mongolia's vast mineral resources are modernizing the country, but nomadic herding thrives.

NUMBER OF COUNTRIES
6

MONGOLIA

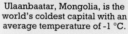

China
Capital city: Beijing
Population: 1,379,302,771
Land area: 3,600,947 mi²
(9,326,410 km²)
Population density:
375 per mi² (145 per km²)

North Korea
Capital city: Pyongyang
Population: 25,248,140
Land area: 46,490 mi²
(120,408 km²)
Population density:
549 per mi² (212 per km²)

Japan
Capital city: Tokyo
Population: 126,451,398
Land area: 140,728 mi²
(364,485 km²)
Population density:
868 per mi² (335 per km²)

South Korea
Capital city: Seoul
Population: 51,181,299
Land area: 37,421 mi²
(96,920 km²)
Population density:
1,334 per mi² (515 per km²)

Mongolia
Capital city: Ulaanbaatar
Population: 3,068,243
Land area: 599,831 mi²
(1,553,556 km²)
Population density:
5 per mi² (2 per km²)

Taiwan
Capital city: Taipei
Population: 23,694,089
Land area: 12,456 mi²
(32,260 km²)
Population density:
1,686 per mi² (651 per km²)

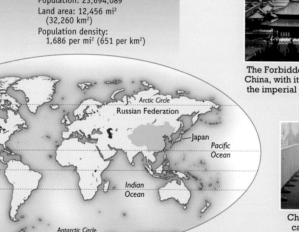

Ulaanbaatar, Mongolia, is the world's coldest capital with an average temperature of -1 °C.

The Forbidden City in Beijing, China, with its 8,704 rooms was the imperial palace until 1912.

China's industrialization has caused dangerous air and water pollution problems.

Flag facts

China
Five—as in the five stars—is a lucky number. Many things in Chinese culture come in fives.

Japan
Known as the "Land of the Rising Sun." The red circle signifies the Sun rising in the east over Japan's 6,852 islands.

Mongolia
The *soyombo* is the national symbol. Its meanings include growth, endurance, harmony, and strength.

North Korea
The red star stands for Communism and patriotic spirit, and the white circle is a symbol of the universe.

South Korea
The yin-yang symbol —meaning unity— sits inside characters meaning heaven, fire, water, and earth.

RUSSIAN FEDERATION

Trans-Siberian Railway

Sea of Okhotsk

Lake Baikal

Irkutsk
Chita
Khabarovsk
Sakhalin

Sühbaatar

Uvs Nuur
Darhan
Erdenet
Ulaanbaatar
Choybalsan

Hulun Nur
Qiqihar
Hegang
Lake Khanka
Sapporo

KURIL ISLANDS (Claimed by Japan)

Hokkaido

Har Us Nuur

MONGOLIA

INNER MONGOLIA

Harbin
Changchun
Jilin
Vladivostok

Fushun
Shenyang
NORTH KOREA

Sea of Japan

Fukushima

JAPAN

Dalandzadgad

Gobi Desert

Haicheng
Pyongyang

Hamhung
Kyoto
Honshu

Tokyo

Baotou
Beijing
Tangshan

SOUTH KOREA
Hiroshima

Kobe
Yokohama

JAPAN

Shijiazhuang
Tianjin
Dalian

Seoul
Busan
Osaka
Nagoya

I N A

Qinghai Hu
Xining
Taiyuan
Zibo

Korea Bay

Yellow Sea

Shikoku

PACIFIC OCEAN

Lanzhou
Xi'an
Jinan
Qingdao
Jeju

Kagoshima
Kyushu

Zhengzhou
Xuzhou

East China Sea

RUNACHAL PRADESH (Claimed by China)

Shanghai
Nanjing
Yangtze River delta

Wuhan

NORTH KOREA

Chengdu
Hangzhou

Okinawa
Ryukyu Islands (Japan)

Chongqing
Nanchang

Changsha
Fuzhou

Taipei

Japan has 1,500 earthquakes a year. The 2011 event caused a nuclear accident at Fukushima.

Kunming
Guiyang

TAIWAN

Taiwan Strait

SOUTH KOREA

Guangzhou
Kaohsiung

MYANMAR

VIETNAM

LAOS

Hong Kong

Gulf of Tonkin

Hainan

TAIWAN

Philippine Sea

North Korea, a highly secretive state, has the fourth-largest army in the world.

THAILAND

South China Sea

PHILIPPINES

Fact
Taiwan regards itself as independent, but China wants it to be reunited with mainland China. Taiwan is a top producer of computer technology.

South Korea's Shinsegae Centum City is the world's largest department store.

Southeast Asia

Southeast Asia includes the mountainous Indochina and Malay peninsulas with their many rivers, and the volcanic and coral islands of the Indonesian and Philippine **archipelagos**. This region sits on the earthquake-prone Ring of Fire. Mostly tropical and rainy, the region's main crops are rice, rubber, tea, and spices. Most of the world's tin comes from Southeast Asia. All of these countries have growing economies.

LAOS

CAMBODIA

Brunei
Capital city: Bandar Seri Begawan
Population: 443,593
Land area: 2,033 mi² (5,265 km²)
Population density:
   189 per mi² (73 per km²)

Cambodia
Capital city: Phnom Penh
Population: 16,204,486
Land area: 68,153 mi² (176,515 km²)
Population density:
   233 per mi² (90 per km²)

Indonesia
Capital city: Jakarta
Population: 260,580,739
Land area: 699,451 mi²
   (1,811,569 km²)
Population density:
   357 per mi² (138 per km²)

Laos
Capital city: Vientiane
Population: 7,126,706
Land area: 89,112 mi² (230,800 km²)
Population density:
   71 per mi² (27 per km²)

Malaysia
Capital city: Kuala Lumpur
Population: 31,381,992
Land area: 126,895 mi² (328,657 km²)
Population density:
   255 per mi² (98 per km²)

Myanmar (Burma)
Capital city: Naypyitaw
Population: 55,123,814
Land area: 252,321 mi² (653,508 km²)
Population density:
   207 per mi² (80 per km²)

Philippines
Capital city: Manila
Population: 104,256,076
Land area: 115,124 mi²
   (298,170 km²)
Population density:
   915 per mi² (353 per km²)

Singapore
Capital city: Singapore
Population: 5,888,926
Land area: 274 mi² (709 km²)
Population density:
   20,192 per mi² (7,796 per km²)

Thailand
Capital city: Bangkok
Population: 68,414,135
Land area: 197,256 mi²
   (510,890 km²)
Population density:
   344 per mi² (133 per km²)

**Timor-Leste
(East Timor)**
Capital city: Dili
Population: 1,291,358
Land area: 5,743 mi²
   (14,874 km²)
Population density:
   202 per mi² (78 per km²)

Vietnam
Capital city: Hanoi
Population: 96,160,163
Land area: 119,719 mi²
   (310,070 km²)
Population density:
   733 per mi² (283 per km²)

NUMBER OF COUNTRIES
11

MYANMAR

THAILAND

Fact
Cutting forests for timber in Thailand, Myanmar, and Laos have destroyed the habitats of tigers and elephants. Thailand has now banned logging.

MALAYSIA

SINGAPORE

INDONESIA

Mandalay
MYANMAR
Naypyitaw
Yangon (Rangoon)
Chiang Mai
Luang Prabang
Hanoi
Vientiane
LAOS
Da Nang
Irrawaddy River delta
THAILAND
Dawei
Bangkok
CAMBODIA
Tonlé Sap
Phnom Penh
VIETNAM
Nha Tran
ANDAMAN ISLANDS (India)
Myeik
Gulf of Thailand
Ho Chi Minh City
Mekong River delta
Andaman Sea
Ko Samui
NICOBAR ISLANDS (India)
Phuket
Kota Bharu
Natuna Islands
Kuala Lumpur
MALAYS
Medan
Strait of Malacca
SINGAPORE
Singapore
Bor
Bangka
Mentawai Islands
Sumatra
I
N
D
Palembang
Jakarta
Java
Surabay
INDIAN
Sou

Arctic Circle
Tropic of Cancer
China
Pacific Ocean
Equator
India
Indian Ocean
Tropic of Capricorn
Australia
Antarctic Circle

Singapore's $1,000 note has the national anthem's lyrics printed on it in microprint.

Indonesia's Pura Tanah Lot, Bali, with its temple is one of Indonesia's 17,508 islands.

Vietnam is the land of motorbikes. They are cheaper than cars and access all the tiny lanes.

Manila, Philippines, has the world's highest population density—111,002 per mi² (42,857 per km²).

RYUKYU ISLANDS (Japan)

TAIWAN

PHILIPPINES

Baguio • *Luzon*
PHILIPPINES
Quezon City •
Manila •
Mindoro • *Samar*

Palawan • *Panay*
Puerto • *Negros*
Princesa
Sulu Sea • Tacloban City

Mindanao
Davao

Philippine Sea

Brunei's Water Village, Bandar Seri Begawan, built 1,000 years ago, is home to 40,000 people.

BRUNEI

YAP ISLANDS (Micronesia)

Palau

VIETNAM

Celebes Sea

Halmahera

BRUNEI
Bandar Seri Begawan

Manado •

N E S I A

Palu • Luwuk •
Molucca Sea
Sulawesi •
Kendari •

Sorong •

Jayapura •

Papua

Ambon •
Buru • *Seram*

Banda Sea

Sumbawa
Flores Sea

Aru Islands

Arafura Sea

Flores
Komodo • *Flores*
Lombok • *Timor* **TIMOR-LESTE**
Sumba Kupang • Dili
Timor Sea

PACIFIC OCEAN

OCEAN

AUSTRALIA

Timor-Leste's major export is coffee. It provides income for a quarter of the population.

TIMOR-LESTE

Flag facts

Brunei
The crest's umbrella symbolizes monarchy; hands, protection; wings, peace; and new moon, Islam.

Myanmar
Yellow is solidarity; green, peace; and red, courage. The star is the country's unity.

Cambodia
Angkor Wat temple is home to Cambodia's Hindu and Buddhist religions. It is the only flag to show a building.

Philippines
When the blue stripe is uppermost, it is a peacetime flag. During war, the red stripe is uppermost.

Indonesia
Known as the "Sacred Red and White." Red is for courage and physical life; white for purity and spiritual life.

Singapore
The five stars represent Singapore's ideals: democracy, peace, progress, justice, and equality.

Laos
The white disk on blue is the moon shining on the Mekong River, the longest river in Southeast Asia.

Thailand
The red is the blood of life; white, the purity of the main religion, Buddhism; and blue, the ruling monarchy.

Malaysia
The Islamic crescent cradles a star that stands for the unity of the 13 states and the federal government.

Timor-Leste
The black triangle refers to the country's recent violent history, and the white star, its desire for peace.

Australia, New Zealand, and Pacific Islands

Australia, New Zealand, and the Pacific Islands, often called Australasia and Oceania, is 25,000 islands spread over nearly 3.3 million square miles (8.5 million km²) of the Pacific Ocean. Australia is the largest country (but the world's smallest continent) and Nauru the smallest. The region is rich in natural and mineral resources, but the smaller Pacific islands—unlike Australia, New Zealand, and Papua New Guinea—have not developed these into industries.

Bikini Atoll, Marshall Islands, is where the first hydrogen bomb was tested in 1952.

NUMBER OF COUNTRIES
14

Fact
Niue is a small self-governing country northeast of New Zealand. It is the largest raised coral atoll on Earth.

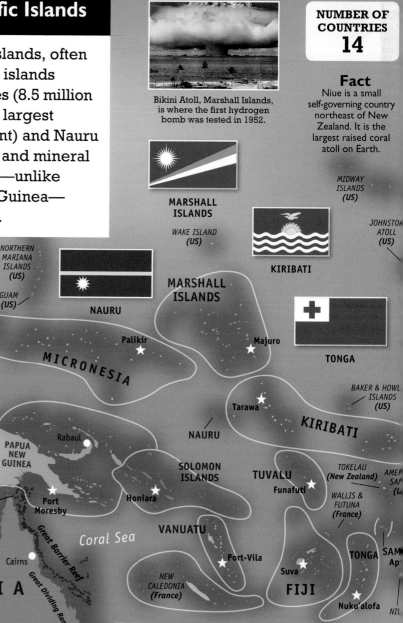

MARSHALL ISLANDS

WAKE ISLAND (US)

MIDWAY ISLANDS (US)

JOHNSTON ATOLL (US)

KIRIBATI

PALAU

MICRONESIA

NORTHERN MARIANA ISLANDS (US)

GUAM (US)

NAURU

MARSHALL ISLANDS

Ngerulmud

Palikir

Majuro

TONGA

PALAU

MICRONESIA

BAKER & HOWL ISLANDS (US)

Tarawa

NAURU

KIRIBATI

Rabaul

PAPUA NEW GUINEA

Port Moresby

SOLOMON ISLANDS

Honiara

TUVALU
Funafuti

TOKELAU (New Zealand)

WALLIS & FUTUNA (France)

AMER SAM (U

PAPUA NEW GUINEA

Timor Sea

Arafura Sea

Cape York

Gulf of Carpentaria

VANUATU

Port-Vila

TONGA

SAM Ap

Melville Island

Darwin

Great Barrier Reef

Coral Sea

Suva

FIJI

Cairns

Nuku'alofa

NIL

INDIAN OCEAN

Broome

North West Cape

AUSTRALIA

Lake Mackay

Alice Springs

Uluru (Ayers Rock)

Lake Eyre North

Lake Torrens

Lake Frome

Great Dividing Range

Brisbane

NEW CALEDONIA (France)

PACIFIC OCEA

Shark Bay

SOLOMON ISLANDS

NORFOLK ISLAND (Australia)

KERMADEC ISLANDS (New Zealand)

AUSTRALIA

Perth

Kalgoorlie

Great Australian Bight

Adelaide

Canberra

Sydney

North Island

Auckland

NEW ZEALAND

Cape Leeuwin

Albany

Kangaroo Island

Melbourne

VANUATU

Tasman Sea

South Island

CHATHAM ISLANDS (New Zealand)

SOUTHERN OCEAN

Bass Strait

TASMANIA

Wellington

Christchurch

Hobart

Invercargill

Stewart Island

Super Pit, Kalgoorlie, Western Australia, is the country's second-largest open-cut gold mine, measuring 2.2 miles (3.5 km long and 1,870 feet (570 m) deep.

Melbourne is one of 10 large cities that are home to 70 percent of Australia's population.

New Zealand's weta is the world's heaviest insect. Its 4-inch (10-cm) body weighs 2.5 ounces (70 g).

NEW ZEALAND

Australia
Capital city: Canberra
Population: 23,232,413
Land area: 2,966,153 mi²
 (7,682,300 km²)
Population density:
 8 per mi² (3 per km²)

Fiji
Capital city: Suva
Population: 920,938
Land area: 7,056 mi²
 (18,274 km²)
Population density:
 122 mi² (47 per km²)

Kiribati
Capital city: Tarawa
Population: 108,145
Land area: 313 mi² (811 km²)
Population density:
 412 per mi² (159 per km²)

 **Marshall Islands**
Capital city: Majuro
Population: 74,539
Land area: 70 mi² (181 km²)
Population density:
 803 per mi² (310 per km²)

Micronesia
Capital city: Palikir
Population: 104,196
Land area: 271 mi² (702 km²)
Population density:
 435 per mi² (168 per km²)

Nauru
Capital city: no official capital
Population: 11,359
Land area: 8 mi² (21 km²)
Population density:
 1,331 per mi² (514 per km²)

New Zealand
Capital city: Wellington
Population: 4,510,327
Land area: 102,138 mi² (264,537 km²)
Population density:
 47 per mi² (18 per km²)

Palau
Capital city: Ngerulmud
Population: 21,431
Land area: 177 mi² (459 km²)
Population density:
 111 per mi² (43 per km²)

Papua New Guinea
Capital city: Port Moresby
Population: 6,909,701
Land area: 174,850 mi² (452,860 km²)
Population density:
 47 per mi² (18 per km²)

Samoa
Capital city: Apia
Population: 200,108
Land area: 1,089 mi² (2,821 km²)
Population density:
 181 per mi² (70 per km²)

Solomon Islands
Capital city: Honiara
Population: 647,581
Land area: 10,805 mi² (27,986 km²)
Population density:
 60 per mi² (23 per km²)

Tonga
Capital city: Nuku'alofa
Population: 106,479
Land area: 277 mi² (717 km²)
Population density:
 363 per mi² (140 per km²)

Tuvalu
Capital city: Funafuti
Population: 11,052
Land area: 10 mi² (26 km²)
Population density:
 1,129 per mi² (436 per km²)

Vanuatu
Capital city: Port-Vila
Population: 282,814
Land area: 4,706 mi² (12,189 km²)
Population density:
 57 per mi² (22 per km²)

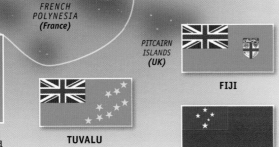
Tuvalu's islands are covered with coconut palms. The dried coconut kernels are exported.

HAWAIIAN ISLANDS
(US)

KINGMAN
REEF
(US)

PALMYRA
ATOLL (US)

JARVIS ISLAND
(US)

KIRIBATI

PACIFIC OCEAN

COOK
ISLANDS
(New
Zealand)

FRENCH
POLYNESIA
(France)

PITCAIRN
ISLANDS
(UK)

FIJI

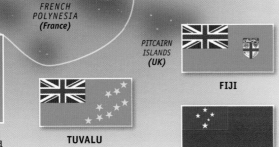
TUVALU

SAMOA

Sri Siva Subramaniya Swami Temple, Nadi, Fiji, is covered with colorful Hindu deities.

Tropic of
Cancer

Hawaii

Equator

Tropic of
Capricorn

Pacific
Ocean

Arctic Circle

Pacific
Ocean

Indian
Ocean

Australia

New
Zealand

Southern Ocean

Antarctic Circle

Flag facts

Fiji
The crest has a British lion holding a cocoa pod, a palm tree, sugar cane, bananas, and a dove of peace.

Samoa
The Southern Cross— a constellation visible only in the southern hemisphere—is shown by the five white stars.

Kiribati
The frigatebird flying over the Pacific Ocean signifies strength. Each sun ray represents one of Kiribati's 17 islands.

Solomon Islands
Here the stars are the five islands of this group; blue, the ocean; and yellow, the sun that bathes the country.

Marshall Islands
The orange and white rays are the group's parallel island chains: Ratak (sunrise) and Ralik (sunset)

Tonga
The red cross symbolizes the Christian faith of the Tongans and Christ's blood and sacrifice.

Nauru
Nauru sits on the Equator—the yellow line—in the middle of the Pacific Ocean— the blue background.

Tuvalu
The Union Jack marks the country's link with Great Britain, and the stars represent Tuvalu's nine islands.

Papua New Guinea
The stars are the Southern Cross; and the bird of paradise, a local tribal symbol.

Vanuatu
The "Y" mimics the shape of this island chain; the pig's tusk, wealth; and the namele leaves, peace.

Flags at a glance

Afghanistan 26	Croatia 22–23	Italy 22–23	Nepal 27	Sri Lanka 27
Albania 22–23	Cuba 8–9	Jamaica 8–9	Netherlands 20	St. Kitts and Nevis 8–9
Algeria 12	Cyprus 24–25	Japan 28–29	New Zealand 32–33	St. Lucia 8–9
Andorra 22	Czechia (Czech Republic) 21	Jordan 24–25	Nicaragua 6–7	St. Vincent and the Grenadines 8–9
Angola 16	Democratic Republic of the Congo 16	Kazakhstan 26	Niger 14–15	State of Palestine 24–25
Antigua and Barbuda 8–9	Denmark 18–19	Kenya 12–13	Nigeria 14–15	Sudan 12–13
Argentina 11	Djibouti 12–13	Kiribati 32–33	North Korea 28–29	Suriname 10
Armenia 24–25	Dominica 8–9	Kosovo 23	Norway 18–19	Swaziland 17
Australia 32–33	Dominican Republic 8–9	Kuwait 24–25	Oman 24–25	Sweden 18–19
Austria 20	Ecuador 10	Kyrgyzstan (Kyrgyz Republic) 26	Pakistan 27	Switzerland 20
Azerbaijan 24–25	Egypt 12–13	Laos 30–31	Palau 32–33	Syria 25
Bahrain 24–25	El Salvador 6–7	Latvia 18–19	Panama 6–7	Taiwan 28–29
Bangladesh 27	Equatorial Guinea 16	Lebanon 24–25	Papua New Guinea 32–33	Tajikistan 26
Barbados 9	Eritrea 12–13	Lesotho 17	Paraguay 11	Tanzania 13
Belarus 21	Estonia 18–19	Liberia 14–15	Peru 10	Thailand 30–31
Belgium 20	Ethiopia 12–13	Libya 12–13	Philippines 30–31	The Bahamas 8
Belize 6–7	Fiji 32–33	Liechtenstein 20	Poland 21	The Gambia 14–15
Benin 14–15	Finland 18–19	Lithuania 18–19	Portugal 22–23	Timor-Leste (East Timor) 30–31
Bhutan 27	France 20	Luxembourg 20	Qatar 24–25	Togo 14–15
Bolivia 11	Gabon 16	Macedonia 23	Republic of the Congo 16	Tonga 32–33
Bosnia and Herzegovina 22–23	Georgia 24–25	Madagascar 13	Romania 21	Trinidad and Tobago 8–9
Botswana 17	Germany 20	Malawi 12–13	Russian Federation 18–19	Tunisia 12–13
Brazil 10	Ghana 14–15	Malaysia 30–31	Rwanda 13	Turkey 24–25
Brunei 30–31	Greece 22–23	Maldives 27	Samoa 32–33	Turkmenistan 26
Bulgaria 21	Grenada 8–9	Mali 14–15	San Marino 23	Tuvalu 32–33
Burkina Faso 14–15	Guatemala 6–7	Malta 23	São Tomé and Príncipe 16	Uganda 13
Burundi 12–13	Guinea 14–15	Marshall Islands 32–33	Saudi Arabia 24–25	Ukraine 21
Cambodia 30–31	Guinea-Bissau 14–15	Mauritania 14–15	Senegal 14–15	United Arab Emirates 25
Cameroon 16	Guyana 10	Mauritius 12–13	Serbia 23	United Kingdom 18–19
Canada 6–7	Haiti 8	Mexico 6–7	Seychelles 13	United States of America 6–7
Cape Verde 14–15	Honduras 6–7	Micronesia 32–33	Sierra Leone 14–15	Uruguay 11
Central African Republic 16	Hungary 21	Moldova 21	Singapore 30–31	Uzbekistan 26
Chad 16	Iceland 18–19	Monaco 20	Slovakia 21	Vanuatu 32–33
Chile 11	India 27	Mongolia 28–29	Slovenia 22–23	Vatican City State 22–23
China 28–29	Indonesia 30–31	Montenegro 23	Solomon Islands 32–33	Venezuela 10
Colombia 10	Iran 24–25	Morocco 12	Somalia 12–13	Vietnam 30–31
Comoros 12–13	Iraq 24–25	Mozambique 12–13	South Africa 17	Yemen 25
Costa Rica 6–7	Ireland 18–19	Myanmar (Burma) 30–31	South Korea 28–29	Zambia 13
Cote d'Ivoire 14–15	Israel 24–25	Namibia 17	South Sudan 12–13	Zimbabwe 12–13
		Nauru 32–33	Spain 22–23	

Learning More

Books

Basher, Simon, *Countries of the World: An Atlas with Attitude*, Kingfisher, 2018

Bednar, Sylvie, *Flags of the World*, Harry N. Abrams, 2009

Colson, Rob, *The Book of Flags: Flags from Around the World and the Stories Behind Them*, Wayland, 2017

Coutts, Lyn, *Flags of the World* (Quick Reference Atlas), Crabtree, 2018

Lonely Planet Kids, *The Travel Book: A journey through every country in the world*, Lonely Planet Kids, 2015

Walker, Robert, *Flag Day* (Celebrations in My World), Crabtree, 2012

Websites

www.atozkidsstuff.com/world.html
Things to know about every country in the world and things to do there. Countries are divided by continent.

www.ducksters.com/geography
Maps, flags, and lots of information about each country.

https://kids.nationalgeographic.com/ search-results/?q=countries
Information about the geography, history, government, nature, and people of the world's countries.

www.kids-world-travel-guide.com/geography-facts.html
Lots of facts and information about the world's continents, countries, and people.

www.sciencekids.co.nz/sciencefacts/countries.html
Provides interesting trivia and information about the countries of the world.

Glossary

abolish To formally put to an end

apartheid A policy of segregation (separation of racial groups) or discrimination (treating someone differently due to their race)

archipelagos A group of islands

Cold War A state of hostility between the Soviet Union and the United States, which consisted of threats, misleading information about each country, and other measures, but not actual war

colonist A settler in or an inhabitant of a colony

colonize To send a group of settlers to a place to establish political control over it

colony A country or area under control of a distant country

descendant A direct relative of someone who lived long ago

direct rule A situation in which the government completely takes over running an area or province

diverse Showing a great deal of variety

dominate To have a commanding influence on

drought A long period of time with very little or no rain

ethnic Describing a population group with a common national or cultural tradition

exploit To use someone or something selfishly for one's own advantage

fauna The animals of a particular region, habitat, or geological period

financial crisis Any situation in which some financial assets (things you own) suddenly lose a larger part of their value

flora The plants of a particular region, habitat, or geological period

ideal Any object or goal, especially one of high or noble character

import A good or service brought into another country from abroad

independence Freedom from the control of another country

instability A condition in which a thing or a procedure is likely to break down

Iron Curtain Imaginary boundary line that divided two political areas: politically free Western Europe and communist Eastern Europe, which was controlled by Russia

landlocked Surrounded by land

liberty The freedom to live life the way one wants, without interference from other people or leaders

mosaic Picture or pattern created by arranging small colored pieces of hard material, such as stone, glass, or tile

natural resources Naturally occurring materials or substances, such as minerals, forests, water, and fertile land, that can be used for economic gain

nomadic Describing people who have no fixed home, but instead move from place to place

patron A god or saint who protects and guides a specific group of people

plantation An estate on which crops such as coffee, sugar, or tobacco are cultivated by workers who live on the property

poverty The state of being very poor and having few belongings

signatories A group of people or country who signs an agreement, such as a treaty

slavery The practice of keeping slaves to do work

spire A tapering cone- or pyramid-shaped structure, such as a church tower

spirit The qualities of courage, energy, strength, and enthusiasm needed to achieve a purpose or goal

territory An area of land controlled by a country or ruler

unique One of a kind; not like anything else

Index

Abu Dhabi 25
Afghanistan 26
Africa 12–17
agriculture 11, 14, 19, 21, 30, 33
Amazon 8
ancient cities 6, 21
Andorra 22
Angkor Wat 31
animals 7, 9, 10, 13, 16, 33
artefacts 12, 23
artworks 22
ASEAN 5
Asia 24–31
Auschwitz, Poland 21
Australasia and Oceania 32–33
Australia 5, 32
Avenida 9 de Julio 11

Bandar Seri Begawan, Brunei 31
Bangladesh 27
battles 19, 20, 23, 24, 31
bauxite 14
bazaars 24
Belize 6, 7
Benin 15
Berbers 12
Bible verses 9
Bibliotheca Alexandrina 13
bicolor flags 4
Bikini Atoll, Marshall Islands 32
borders 4
Brazil 10
Buddhism 27, 31
Buenos Aires 11

Cameroon 16
Canada 6–7
cantons 4
Caribbean 8–9
Catalonia, Spain 22
Central America 6
chevrons 4
China 28
Christianity 4, 25, 33
coats of arms 16, 21
coffee beans 31
coldest capital city 28
colonization 12
Conakry, Guinea 14
concentration camps 21
crests 7, 10, 11, 20, 31, 33
Croatia 22
crosses 4, 5, 19, 20, 21, 23, 33
crowns 20

Cuba 8
currency 30

danger flags 5
Dead Sea 24
deserts 11, 12–13, 15, 17, 24, 28
distress flags 5
Dominica 9
dragonblood trees 25

earthquakes 29, 30
Ebola virus 14
Egypt 13
Elmina Castle 14
endangered species 16, 30
Europe 18–23
European Union 5, 20
explorers 23

Falkland Islands 11
favelas 10
fess 4
fields (or ground) 4
Fiji 33
film industry 15
financial hardships 21, 22, 23
fishing boats 23
fjords 18
flag facts 7, 9, 11, 12, 15, 16, 17, 20, 21, 23, 24, 26, 27, 28, 31, 33
flooding 27
fly 4
Forbidden City, China 28
forest destruction 30
France 20
freedom 7, 11, 12, 15

Gabon masks 16
Ganges River 27
Ganvie village 15
Ghana 14
Gobustan, Azerbaijan 25
government 9, 15, 27, 31
Grand Inga Dam 16
Great Mosque of Djenné 14
Greece 23
Greek crosses 4
Grenada 9
Guinea 14

Haiti 8
half-mast 4
halyards 4
highest population density 31
Hinduism 10, 27, 31, 33
hoists 4

Hungary 21
hydrogen bomb testing 32

Iceland 18
imports 8, 17
Inca Empire 11
independence 7, 9, 10, 15, 17, 22, 29
India 27
international flags 5
International Red Cross 5, 20
Ireland 18
Islam 12, 15, 25, 26, 27, 31
Istanbul, Turkey 24
Italy 22

Japan 29
Judaism 21, 24, 25

Kazakhstan 26
Kumbh Mela 27

Lagos, Nigeria 15
land and forests 9, 10, 11, 15, 19, 24
languages spoken 18
Lesotho 17
liberty 7, 9, 11, 12, 16, 23
Los Angeles 6
Luxembourg 20

Madagascar 13
Mali 14
Malta 23
Mandela, Nelson 17
Manila, Philippines 31
Mayan civilization 6
Melbourne, Australia 32
mining 12, 32
mixed-race families 18
mosaics 24
mosques 14, 26
mountain gorillas 16
mountains 9, 11, 21, 22

national symbols 4, 7, 17, 23, 24, 27, 28
NATO 5
natural resources 11, 15, 17, 28, 32
Netherlands 20
neutral country 20
New Zealand 32
North America 6–9
North Korea 29
Norway 18
nuclear energy 20
nutmeg 9

Ocho Rios, Jamaica 8
oil and gas 6, 9, 21, 26
Olympic Games 5

pales 4
palls 4
Pamir Highway 26
Panama Canal 7
Paphos, Cyprus 24
Paralympic Games 5
parts of a flag 4
patterns 4
peace 7, 12, 24, 31, 33
peanut harvesting 14
Pitons 9
Plovdiv, Bulgaria 21
pollution 28
Pope 23
poverty 6, 10, 14, 16, 21, 23, 26, 27
protocol 4
public transportation 19
Pura Tanah Lot, Bali 30

quarterlies 4

rainforests 9, 10
ratios 5
records 5
refugees 13
religions 10, 12, 15, 19, 23, 24, 25, 26, 27, 31, 33
Ring of Fire 30
rock engravings 25
Running of the Bulls 22
Russia 19

saltires 4
Samarkand mosque 26
Santiago, Chile 11
São Tomé and Príncipe 16
Scandinavian crosses 4
Secretariat of the Antarctic Treaty 5
Senegal 14
shapes 5, 27
ships' flags 4, 5
Sialkot, Pakistan 27
sifakas 13
Silk Road 26
Singapore 30
sizes 5
ski resorts 17
slavery 8, 9, 14
soccer balls 27
Somalia 13
South America 10–11
Southern Cone 11
Spain 22
special rules 4
Sri Siva Subramaniya Swami Temple 33

staff ornaments 4
stars 7, 9, 10, 12, 15, 16, 23, 24, 27, 28, 31, 33
state flags 5
suns 7, 9, 11, 12, 15, 17, 23, 26, 28, 33
Super Pit 32
Suriname 10
Swaziland 17
Sweden 18
Switzerland 20
symmetrical crosses 4

Taiwan 29
Tajikistan 26
Tallinn, Estonia 19
temples 30, 31, 33
thermal waters 21
threatened species 6
Timor-Leste 31
tourism 8, 9, 21, 22
Trans-Siberian Railway 19
trash recycling 18
Trinidad and Tobago 9
trucks 4
Tuvalu 33

Ulaanbaatar, Mongolia 28
UNESCO 5
UNICEF 5
unique flags 11, 27
United Arab Emirates 25
United Kingdom 18
United Nations 4, 5
United States of America (USA) 5, 6–7
unity 7, 10, 12, 15, 17, 20, 23
upside down flags 4, 31
Uruguay 11
Uzbekistan 26

Venezuela 10
vexillology 4
Vietnam 31
village on stilts 15
volcanoes 7, 18, 19

Water Village 31
weapons 12, 24
weta 32
White House 7
wind power 11
World War Two 21

Yemen 25

Zambia 12
Zlatni Rat Beach 22